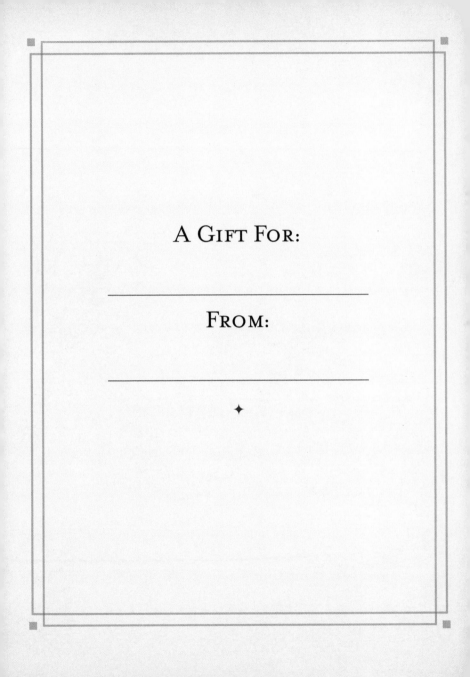

A GIFT FOR:

_____

FROM:

_____

✦

This edition published in 2014 by Hallmark Gift Books,
a division of Hallmark Cards, Inc., Kansas City, MO
64141 under license from Joey Green.
Visit us on the Web at Hallmark.com.

Editorial Director: Delia Berrigan
Editor: Kim Schworm Acosta
Art Director: Chris Opheim
Illustrator and Designer: Brian Pilachowski
Production Designer: Bryan Ring

ISBN: 978-1-59530-863-4
BOK2159

Printed and bound in China
JUL14

HAPPY ACCIDENTS

THE STORY BEHIND BLUE JEANS, POTATO CHIPS, PENICILLIN, & 186 MORE CHANCE DISCOVERIES THAT CHANGED THE WORLD

JOEY GREEN

Hallmark

OTHER BOOKS BY JOEY GREEN

Contrary to Popular Belief

Joey Green's Cleaning Magic

Joey Green's Amazing Pet Cures

Joey Green's Magic Health Remedies

Weird & Wonderful Christmas

The Ultimate Mad Scientist Handbook

Joey Green's Kitchen Magic

Dumb History: The Stupidest Mistakes Ever Made

Selling Out: If Famous Authors Wrote Advertising

Joey Green's Fix-it Magic

Joey Green's Gardening Magic

You Know You've Reached Middle Age If…

Clean It! Fix It! Eat It!

Marx & Lennon: The Parallel Sayings

"Man plans. God laughs."

—*Yiddish proverb*

INTRODUCTION

"Accident is the name of the greatest of all inventors."

—*Mark Twain*

Necessity may be the mother of invention, but all too often the father is dumb luck. The telephone, the phonograph, the Frisbee, the microwave oven, safety glass, and Super Glue all owe their existence to chance mishaps. Some of the world's greatest archaeological finds—Venus de Milo, Machu Picchu, Pompeii, and the Terracotta Warriors—were discovered by accident. Sheer happenstance gave the world Rogaine, smallpox vaccine, eggs Benedict, blue jeans, and Silly Putty.

But recognizing a blessing in disguise can pose a tough challenge. Christopher Columbus went to his grave convinced that he had found a shortcut to India. He stubbornly refused to accept the fact that he had discovered something much more profound—an entirely new world.

When your plans go awry, the universe usually has something much better in store for you—if you're open-minded to the possibilities unfolding serendipitously before you. "The Chinese use two brush strokes to write the word *crisis*," explained John F. Kennedy in a 1959 speech in Indianapolis. "One brush stroke stands for danger; the other for opportunity. In a crisis, be aware of the danger—but recognize the opportunity." In other words, if you let go of your expectations, something far more wonderful usually presents itself—the unexpected.

John Lennon summed it up best in his song "Beautiful Boy (Darling Boy)": "Life is what happens to you while you're busy making other plans." The stories in this book attest to that. Accidentally, of course.

BUBBLE GUM

n 1928, Walter E. Diemer, a 23-year-old accountant working for the Fleer Chewing Gum Company in Philadelphia, tinkered with new gum recipes in his spare time. One batch turned out less sticky and more elastic than regular chewing gum, stretching easily. "It was an accident," Diemer told the *Lancaster Intelligencer Journal* in 1996. "I was doing something else and ended up with something with bubbles." The now customary pink color was also serendipitous. It was the only food coloring Diemer could find in the company lab at the time.

Envisioning the possibilities, Diemer brought a five-pound chunk of the pink, popping bubble gum to a grocery store to be sold in small pieces. The gum sold out by the end of the afternoon.

The Fleer Chewing Gum Company marketed Diemer's invention as Dubble Bubble for a penny apiece. Diemer taught the company's salesmen how to blow bubbles so they could demonstrate the gum's unique property. The innovative accountant rose to become a senior vice president of the company. While he never received any royalties for his invention, he felt tremendously rewarded knowing he had created something that made kids happy around the world.

COCA-COLA

On May 8, 1886, Atlanta pharmacist John Styth Pemberton—inventor of Globe Flower Cough Syrup, Indian Queen Magic Hair Dye, Triplex Liver Pills, and Extract of Styllinger—developed a thick syrup from sugar water, a kola nut extract, and coca as a headache cure. Pemberton brought his new syrup elixir to Jacob's Drug Store where druggist Willis Venable added carbonated water.

Pemberton marketed the soft drink as "a valuable  Brain Tonic," and bookkeeper Frank M. Robinson, one of Pemberton's four partners, suggested naming the elixir Coca-Cola after two of the main ingredients: the coca leaf and the kola nut—spelling *kola* with a *c* for the sake of alliteration. Robinson wrote the name in his bookkeeper's Spenserian script, much the way it appears today.

Two years later, fellow Atlanta pharmacist Asa Candler, convinced that drinking Coca-Cola relieved his migraine headaches, purchased the rights to the formula for $2,300. Candler kept the formula a well-guarded secret, and on January 31, 1893, he trademarked the name.

BOTOX

n the 1970s, while trying to develop a cure for crossed eyes, San Francisco ophthalmologist Dr. Alan B. Scott injected a purified strain of *botulinum toxin* into the hyperactive ocular muscles of a cross-eyed monkey. The toxin, originally developed for possible use as a biological weapon, impaired the muscles that pulled inward, re-aligning the eyes. Dr. Scott named the drug Oculinum, combining the words *ocular* and *botulinum*. In 1991, the California pharmaceutical company Allergan bought the rights to Oculinum for $4.5 million and renamed it Botox, by mashing together the words *botulinum* and *toxin*.

A year later, Canadian ophthalmolo-gist Dr. Jean Carruthers noticed that Botox also eliminated wrinkles in her eye-spasm patients for several months.

Together with her dermatologist husband, Carruthers tested Botox on their receptionist, Cathy Bickerton. Botox would soon change the face of cosmetic medicine.

Doctors now use Botox to treat hundreds of disorders including migraines, speech impediments, drooling, and muscle spasms. Dr. Scott regrets having sold his discovery to the drug company. "If I had held on to Botox," he told *The Times of India* in 2012, "maybe I could have made a billion dollars a year now."

Ironically, the inventive ophthalmologist cannot use Botox to smooth his own wrinkles. Before he started working with the dangerous botulinum toxin, he had to be vaccinated against it. Lamented Dr. Scott: "Botox will not work on me."

TERRACOTTA WARRIORS

On the morning of March 29, 1974, six peasant farmers from the village of Xiyang in the People's Republic of China set out with picks and shovels to dig a well in a dusty field approximately one mile east of the tomb mound of Qin Shi Huangdi, the first emperor of China. After several days, when the hole was thirteen feet deep and ten feet in diameter, two farmers digging at the bottom hit something hard with a shovel.

The farmers kneeled down and brushed away the dirt to reveal a life-size statue of a human soldier made from baked clay called terracotta. The farmers loaded their finds into a three-wheeled cart and rolled it to the village of Xiyang to show the authorities.

A few months later, a team of archaeologists began excavating the area, and after several weeks, they unearthed a vast room under the field, which contained 6,000 life-size terracotta warriors and six four-horse chariots in eleven rows. Each warrior had unique facial features, an individualized expression, and a distinct hairstyle and headgear, suggesting that each soldier was individually shaped by hand and perhaps modeled after actual soldiers. Two years later, archaeologists found a second chamber containing another 1,400 terracotta warriors and horses, and shortly afterward, they unearthed a third vault containing 73 terracotta warriors guarding terracotta commanders riding in terracotta chariots.

Archaeologists believe these underground chambers of terracotta figures are part of Qin Shi Huangdi's tomb complex and constitute a spirit city, where the spirits of the dead were believed to live on to protect the emperor in the afterlife. Qin Shi Huangdi died in 210 B.C.E., dating the terracotta warriors, if they were crafted concurrently, to that time.

Today, a covered museum sits over the three chambers so visitors can view the astounding terracotta army.

CHICKEN CHOLERA VACCINE

n 1879, French chemist Louis Pasteur decided to seek a cure for chicken cholera, a disease that destroyed French poultry farms. Pasteur had recently discovered that microbes caused the fermentation of wine and that pro-

tozoan-infested grain caused a disease that killed silkworms. Knowing that chickens injected with a culture of cholera microbes typically died within twenty-four hours, he started his research by preparing a culture of cholera microbes— before leaving for a three-month summer vacation.

After returning from vacation, Pasteur injected chickens with the culture he had prepared three months earlier, figuring the culture would produce the disease in the hens. To his surprise, the chickens remained unaffected and healthy. He then injected the healthy chickens with a freshly prepared batch of cholera culture. Again, the hens failed to develop cholera and die within the usual twenty-four hours after exposure.

Pasteur realized that he had accidentally discovered the vaccine for chicken cholera—and a previously unknown scientific fact: Weakened microbes can be used as a vaccine to bestow immunity without producing the disease. Based on this premise, Pasteur went on to produce vaccines against anthrax in 1881 and rabies in 1885.

CELLOPHANE

One day in 1900, Swiss chemist Jacques E. Brandenberger was sitting in a café when a hapless customer at a nearby table accidentally spilled a glass of red wine, which soaked into the tablecloth. While watching the waiter change the stained tablecloth, Brandenberger set his heart on inventing a liquid-repelling, stain-resistant tablecloth for restaurants.

Having worked as a textile engineer, Brandenberger  figured he could realize his dream by applying a flexible, waterproof coating to a tablecloth. He began experimenting with cellulose (a derivative of wood pulp), which, when treated with acid, yields a film that can be manipulated. He applied liquefied cellulose to the cloth and then treated the cellulose-coated fabric with a wide variety of substances. But his experiments merely produced a stiff tablecloth with a plastic coating that peeled off easily.

Realizing the resultant sheet of plastic coating was clear, flexible, and waterproof, Brandenberger named the film cellophane by combining the words *cellulose* and *diaphane* (Greek for "transparent"). He patented the process for making the material in 1912 and began manufacturing the film for use as the eyepiece in gas masks. In 1917, Brandenberger assigned his patent to his company, La Cellophane Société Anonyme. Five years later, the chemical company DuPont bought the exclusive rights from La Cellophane to manufacture and distribute cellophane in the United States.

Brandenberger's original cellophane repelled water, but water vapor still penetrated the film. DuPont scientist Hale Charch solved that problem, creating the first true industrial film and making convenient sterile packaging for food and medical supplies possible for the first time.

POTATO CHIPS

n 1853, a guest at the elegant Moon Lake Lodge resort in Saratoga Springs, New York, sent his order of French fries back to the kitchen several times because he wanted them cut thinner and cooked more thoroughly. At the time, the Moon Lake Lodge prepared French fries by slicing the potatoes lengthwise and frying the disks lightly to be eaten with a fork.

A chef named George Crum, the son of an African-American father and Native-American mother, agitated by the complaint, sliced the pota-toes as thin as possible, fried them to a crisp in grease, topped them with salt, and sent them back out to the guest.

Astonishingly, the guest loved Crum's potato chips. When other guests began asking for them as well, the Moon Lake Lodge added "Saratoga Chips" to the menu. In 1860, Crum opened his own restaurant, Crumbs House, near Saratoga Lake and placed a basket of potato chips on every table.

Crum never patented his invention or attempted wide-scale distribution. Other aspiring snack food entrepreneurs turned potato chips into an international phenomenon.

SCOTCH TAPE

n 1925, the automobile industry, eager to satisfy Americans' cravings for two-tone cars, had difficulty making a clean, sharp edge where one color met another. Richard Drew, a laboratory employee working with the abrasives used to make sandpaper at the Minnesota Mining and Manufacturing Company (better known as 3M), developed a two-inch-wide strip of paper tape coated with a rubber-based adhesive. To cut costs, Drew coated the tape with only a strip of glue one-quarter inch wide along the edges, instead of covering the entire two-inch width. Unfortunately, the tape failed to hold properly, and the automobile painters purportedly told the 3M

salesman to "Take this tape back to those Scotch bosses of yours and tell them to put adhesive all over the tape, not just on the edges." The 3M company complied, but when the salesman returned to the automobile paint shop, a painter derogatorily asked him if he was still selling that "Scotch" masking tape, launching a trade name based on an ethnic slur denoting stinginess. The name, like the improved tape, stuck.

In 1929, the Flaxlinum Company asked 3M to develop a water- and odor-proof tape to seal the wrapping on insulation slabs in railroad refrigerator cars. Drew coated cellophane, a new moisture-proof packaging material developed by DuPont, with a rubber-based adhesive, which, while not strong enough for insulation slabs, was marketed to the trade as "the only natural, transparent, quick seal for 'Cellophane'" and named it Scotch Tape, embracing the derogatory epithet.

TABASCO PEPPER SAUCE

I n 1862, when Union troops entered New Orleans, Louisiana, banker Edmund McIlhenny fled with his wife, Mary Avery McIlhenny, to her family's plantation home on Avery Island, an island of solid rock salt approximately 140 miles west of New Orleans and the site of one of America's first rock salt mines. The next year, when Union forces invaded the island and destroyed the salt mining buildings and equipment, the McIlhennys sought refuge in Texas.

After the Civil War, Edmund McIlhenny and his wife returned to Avery Island to find the neglected mansion and, according to folklore, a crop of capsicum hot peppers. Determined to turn the peppers into income,

McIlhenny made a pepper sauce by mixing crushed peppers and salt in crockery jars and letting the concoction age for thirty days. He then added "the best French wine vinegar" and let the mixture age for another thirty days. He strained the fiery red sauce, poured it into several small cologne bottles capped with sprinkler fitments, and gave samples to his family and friends. In 1869, encouraged by the response, McIlhenny sent 658 bottles of his pepper sauce under the trademark Tabasco—named after the state of Tabasco in southern Mexico—to a carefully selected group of southern wholesalers, and by the mid-1870s, he was selling thousands of bottles a year.

McIlhenny Company uses the same process to make Tabasco Pepper Sauce today that Edmund McIlhenny devised in 1868 and currently ages the mash for three years. Avery Island remains the headquarters for the company, which is owned and operated by direct descendants of Edmund McIlhenny. As of 2013, Tabasco Pepper Sauce was distributed in 165 markets and labeled in twenty-two languages.

THE GNOSTIC GOSPELS

In December 1945, Egyptian farmer Muhammad Ali al-Samman and his brothers rode their camels from the town of Naj Hammadi to the Jabal al-Tarif, a mountain honeycombed with caves, to dig up rich soil to use as fertilizer for their crops. Near a boulder, they struck a red, earthenware jar roughly three feet tall. Hoping to find treasure, Muhammad Ali smashed open the jar with his mattock and inside found thirteen leather-bound papyrus books. He carried them to his home in al-Qasr, where his mother used some of them as kindling to light their outdoor clay oven.

A few weeks later, Muhammad Ali and his brothers murdered the man who they claimed had killed

their father. Fearing that the police would search his home and discover the antiquities, Muhammad Ali gave one of the papyrus books, written in Coptic, an Egyptian language related to Greek, to a local Coptic priest. A local history teacher suspected the book might be valuable and sent it to a friend in Cairo, who sold it on the black market. Egyptian government officials bought back the book, confiscated eleven bound books that Muhammad Ali had given to an unsavory antiquities dealer in Cairo, and returned them to the Coptic Museum in Cairo. The thirteenth book was smuggled out of Egypt and put up for sale in America. Dutch professor Gilles Quispel convinced the Jung Foundation in Zurich, Switzerland, to buy it.

Muhammad Ali had smashed the earthenware jar hoping for treasure, but the farmer never realized what a true treasure he found. The thirteen books, dated between 350 and 500 C.E., contain fifty-two texts, including the Gospel of Thomas, the Gospel of Philip, the Gospel of Truth, the Holy Book of the Great Invisible Spirit, the Secret Book of John, the Secret Book of James, the Book of Thomas, the Dialog of the Savior, and the Second Discourse of Great Seth.

VULCANIZED RUBBER

The indigenous people of South America discovered that the milky fluid found in the *Hevea brasiliensis* tree coagulates into a waterproof gum when exposed to air. Unfortunately, this latex became soft and sticky at higher temperatures and stiff and brittle at lower temperatures, making it relatively useless for product development.

In 1770, English chemist Joseph Priestley discovered that a wad of this latex could be used to erase pencil markings by rubbing, earning the substance the name *rubber*. In the 1830s, American inventor Charles Goodyear, obsessed by the idea of making rubber impervious to temperature changes, feverishly experimened to figure out a way to treat rubber by adding drying agents.

In February 1839, after years of failed experimentation, Goodyear wandered into the general store in Woburn, Massachusetts, to show off his latest rubber-and-sulfur formula to the men hanging around the cracker barrel. When Goodyear excitedly waved his fistful of sticky gum in the air, it accidentally flew from his hand and landed on the sizzling-hot potbellied stove. Goodyear scraped the rubber off the stove to discover that the rubber had charred like leather rather than melting like molasses. The heat and sulfur had turned the "elastic gum" into "weatherproof rubber."

Goodyear ultimately discovered that pressurized steam applied for four to six hours at around 270 degrees Fahrenheit stabilized the rubber formula. In 1844, he received a patent for his process, which he called "vulcanization," after the Roman god of fire, Vulcan. Goodyear died $200,000 in debt in 1860. Neither he nor his family was ever connected with the Goodyear Tire & Rubber Company in Akron, Ohio—founded in 1898 by Frank A. Seiberling and named in honor of the man who discovered vulcanization.

PETRI DISH

n 1881, German doctor Robert Koch, conducting research at the Imperial Health Bureau in Berlin, noticed that a slice of potato left on a bench in his laboratory was covered with spots of different colors. He placed a spot from the potato on a slide, examined it under a microscope, and discovered that the microorganisms on the spot were all the same. He examined a sample from a different-colored spot through his microscope and discovered that the microorganisms, while all the same, differed from those in the first spot.

Koch quickly realized that each spot contained a colony of a specific microorganism, meaning that the potato provided the perfect environment for colonies of distinct microbes to grow separately.

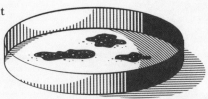

Up until this point, scientists grew bacteria in flasks containing a nutrient broth, producing a variety of microorganisms mixed together and difficult to separate.

Koch set about to develop a more practical medium than the potato for culturing microbes. He added gelatin to the extant liquid broth to create a solid medium, but, when placed in an incubator, the gelatin melted. In 1882, Fanny Hesse, the wife of a colleague who had been stationed in the Dutch East Indies, suggested that Koch use agar, a gelling compound derived from Japanese seaweed that she had used to make jam. In 1887, Koch's assistant, Richard Julius Petri, designed a shallow, round, flat-bottomed glass dish with a cover to hold the agar. Scientists could then streak a throat swab or other clinical specimen over the gelatinous medium in the newly devised Petri dish or "agar plate," incubate it at body temperature, and grow colonies of microbes, which could then be isolated and identified.

TEA

Legend holds that Chinese emperor Shen Nung discovered tea in 2737 B.C.E. The emperor was purportedly resting beneath a *Camellia sinensis* tree on a spring day while his servant boiled drinking water. (Shen Nung, a scholar and celebrated herbalist considered the father of traditional Chinese medicine, drank only boiled water for the sake of hygiene.) The wind stirred and some leaves from  the tree fell into the pot of boiling water. The leaves colored the water and gave it a captivating aroma. Shen Nung decided to taste the hot beverage that his servant had inadvertently brewed and found the tea refreshing and revitalizing.

More than 4,600 years later, at the 1904 World's Fair in St. Louis, Missouri, Englishman Richard Blechynden, a special commissioner representing British tea companies, attempted to publicize India and Ceylon tea in the United States by selling hot Indian black tea. When exceptionally hot weather devastated his sales and fairgoers sought refreshing cold drinks, Blechynden cleverly filled glasses with ice and poured the hot tea over it, creating an instant hit at the World's Fair. Blechynden unwittingly popularized the summer tradition of iced tea, producing a boon for the tea industry.

Today, 85 percent of the tea consumed by Americans is iced.

NOXZEMA

n 1914, pharmacist Dr. George Bunting combined medication and vanishing cream in the prescription room of his Baltimore drugstore to create "Dr. Bunting's Sunburn Remedy." He mixed, heated, and poured the skin cream into little blue jars from a huge coffee pot. When other druggists began ordering his sunburn remedy for their customers, Bunting decided to devote all his energies to marketing the skin cream.

Shortly afterward, a customer told Bunting, "Your sunburn cream sure knocked my eczema," inspiring Bunting to change the name of "Dr. Bunting's Sunburn Remedy" to "Noxzema"—a clever combination of the misspelled word *knocks*

and the last two syllables of the word *eczema*. After all, figured Bunting, more people suffer from eczema than sunburn pain.

In 1920, Bunting opened the first Noxzema "factory" in a tiny house in Baltimore. Bunting's fellow druggists helped finance the Noxzema Chemical Company by placing Noxzema in their stores and buying shares of stock in the company—usually for one hundred dollars or less. By 1925, sales reached $100,000, and Bunting launched Noxzema nationally, starting with New York City in 1926, followed by Chicago and the Midwest in 1928, the South and Pacific Coast in 1930, and the prairie and Rocky Mountain states in 1938. With national distribution in place, Noxzema began advertising on national radio broadcasts of "Professor Quiz." Sales jumped 40 percent in one season, and Noxzema began expanding into shaving cream, suntan lotions, and cold cream.

POOL OF SILOAM

n the fall of 2004, the central sewage line for Jerusalem's Old City got blocked and backed up. Workers repairing the damaged sewage pipe in the nearby village of Silwan unearthed two steps of a stone staircase. As soon as Eli Shukron of the Israel Antiquities Authority saw the two uncovered steps, he halted the work and called in archaeologist Ronny Reich of the University of Haifa. Convinced that they had found the biblical Pool of Siloam, a freshwater reservoir where the Gospel of John reports that Jesus cured a man blind since birth, Shukron and Reich ex-

cavated the site as quickly as possible so the sewer could be repaired before the winter rainy season commenced.

The archaeologists uncovered three tiers of stone stairs leading into a pool roughly 225 feet long—fed water by Hezekiah's Tunnel. Scholars had previously declared the Pool of Siloam a creation of the gospel writer. Built in the first century B.C.E., the pool was laid waste by the Roman emperor Titus around 70 C.E.

The pool is the second of three known Pools of Siloam. Archaeologists believe that the first Pool of Siloam, a reservoir built in the eighth century B.C.E. by Judean king Hezekiah and connected to the Gihon Spring by a 1,750-foot-long tunnel under the City of David, was destroyed in 586 B.C.E. when Babylonian king Nebuchadnezzar decimated Jerusalem. The third Pool of Siloam, a reconstruction built in the fifth century C.E. by Byzantine empress Eudocia, stands roughly 200 yards from the second Pool of Siloam.

FRISBEE

I n 1871, William Russell Frisbie moved to Bridgeport, Connecticut, and opened a bakery called the Frisbie Pie Company. He sold a wide assortment of bakery goods, including pies packed in lightweight tins embossed with his family name. Children in Bridgeport tossed the empty pie tins as a game, which made its way to college campuses—most notably nearby Yale University, where students yelled "Frisbie!" to warn innocent bystanders of an incoming pie tin.

In 1948, Walter Frederick Morrison, a Los Angeles building inspector determined to capitalize on Hollywood's  obsession with UFOs, designed a lightweight plastic disk, based on the Frisbie bakery's pie tins, but changed the name to Flyin' Saucer to avoid any potential legal entanglements. Morrison sold the rights to the Wham-O Manufacturing Co. of San Gabriel, California, and on January 13, 1957, Americans were introduced to the Frisbee. (Wham-O changed the name of the toy back to its more popular moniker, cleverly altering the spelling to sidestep trademark hassles.) Although the Frisbie Pie Company went out of business in 1958, the Frisbee became one of the most popular and iconic toys of all time.

ARCHIMEDES' PRINCIPLE

In the third century B.C.E., Hiero, the king of Syracuse, commissioned a goldsmith to fashion a royal crown from a bar of pure gold. When Hiero received the crown, he wondered whether the goldsmith had mixed a less valuable metal, such as silver or copper, with some of the gold the king had provided—and then kept the leftover gold for himself. Hiero summoned the Greek mathematician Archimedes to find the answer.

Archimedes realized that if he could determine the volume of the crown, he could calculate whether the crown was the same volume as the gold the king had supplied to the goldsmith.

If the goldsmith had substituted another metal for some of the gold, the crown's volume would be greater than the original volume of gold. But Archimedes had no idea how to measure the volume of the crown.

While bathing at the public baths, Archimedes noticed that when he immersed his body in the water, the water level rose. When he emerged from the bath, the water level fell accordingly. The volume of his body, Archimedes realized, displaced an equal volume of water. All he had to do was place the king's crown in a bowl filled with water and then measure the volume of the displaced water. Exhilarated, Archimedes ran home from the public baths without his clothes, shouting "Eureka! Eureka!" He had developed the law of physics known today as Archimedes' principle.

Unfortunately for the goldsmith, the volume of the crown proved far greater than it should have been, and Hiero had him executed.

BAG BALM

n 1899, John L. Norris bought the formula for Bag Balm, a salve created by a Vermont druggist in Wells River to soften cow udders—also known as "bags"—made sore from milking. Made from petrolatum, lanolin, and an antiseptic, Bag Balm speeds the relief of bruised, sore, or injured teats.

Dairy farmers soon discovered that a dab of Bag Balm

also soothed minor cuts and abrasions and dry cracked paw pads of the family dog. The farmers' wives noticed how smooth their husband's fingers had become after using the product. Since then, people have used Bag Balm to relieve psoriasis, dermatitis, cracked fingers, burns, saddle sores, sunburn, pimples, bedsores, and radiation burns. The product's popularity soared primarily through word of mouth.

In 1937, Admiral Richard Byrd took a can of Bag Balm on his trip to the North Pole to help protect his skin against the harsh climate. During World War II, allied troops used it to prevent weapons from corroding. After the terrorist attacks of September 11, 2001, rescue teams at Ground Zero applied Bag Balm to the paws of cadaver-sniffing dogs searching the rubble of the World Trade Center.

MARTIN & LEWIS

n September 1944, Catskills comedian Jerry Lewis and his friend, Sonny King, bumped into singer Dean Martin (then the host of his own radio show on WMCA) on the corner of 49th Street and Broadway in New York City. King introduced Lewis to Martin.

After that, Martin and Lewis frequently crossed each other's paths at various clubs. In March 1946, the Havana Club booked Jerry Lewis and Dean Martin as separate acts to appear on the same bill. The comedian and singer visited each other's acts, often joking out loud during the other's performance.

In July 1946, Lewis's agent booked him into the 500 Club in Atlantic City, New Jersey, where Martin was again booked on the same bill. Martin would go on first and sing, and then Lewis would follow with his comedy routine. "We started horsing around with each other's acts," Martin told the *Saturday Evening Post* in 1961. "That's how the team Martin and Lewis started. We'd do anything that came to our minds, anything at all."

Martin and Lewis would perform their own routines and then join each other as a twosome at the end of their shows. When Martin sang, Lewis interrupted with zany clowning. They traded insults, ad-libbed, and acted like manic mad men. The audience loved it. "We lasted six weeks at the Club 500," recalled Martin. "It was wonderful."

In January 1947, Martin and Lewis launched their careers as a full-fledged team. They were soon playing to packed nightclubs and theaters across the country and quickly became the most popular comedy team in the nation—breaking records in nightclubs and on radio and television. After starring together in seventeen movies, they split up their act in 1956.

n 1869, while studying at University College in London, 22-year-old Alexander Graham Bell became intrigued by the writings of German physicist Hermann von Helmholtz. In his thesis *On the Sensations of Tone*, Helmholtz declared that a combination of electrical tuning forks and resonators could produce vowel sounds. Unable to read German, Bell misinterpreted Helmholtz as stating that vowel sounds could be transmitted *over a wire*—rather than *by a wire*. Three years later in Boston, Massachusetts, Bell began his attempt to invent what he called the "harmonic telegraph," a way to transmit multiple messages simultaneously by sending musical chords over the telegraph wire.

On June 2, 1875, Bell's mechanic, Thomas Watson, working in the transmitter room

and trying to free a reed that had been too tightly wound to the pole of its electromagnet, produced a twang heard by Bell, who had been working in the receiving room. Realizing that the complex overtones and timbre of the twang were similar to those in the human voice, Bell became convinced that he could transmit human speech over a wire. Shortly afterward, he discovered that a vibrating wire partially immersed in a conducting liquid, like mercury, could be made to produce an undulating current.

On March 10, 1876, as he and Watson attempted to test this finding, Bell knocked over the battery acid they were using as a conducting liquid and shouted, "Mr. Watson, come here. I want you!" Watson, working in the next room, heard Bell's voice through the wire, marking the world's first telephone call. Later that year, Bell introduced the telephone to the world at the Centennial Exhibition in Philadelphia.

SULFA DRUGS

n 1930, Eric Baines, a chemist at the British pharmaceutical company May & Baker, prepared a bottle of the
organic compound aminopyridine for a colleague who
left the company before using it. That sample stood on a
shelf untouched for seven years—until one day in October
1937, someone in the laboratory noticed the dusty bottle
sitting in the cupboard and decided to test the compound
to create a more effective analog of sulfanilamide—a
synthetic antibacterial compound. Chemists at May &
Baker had spent the previous three years testing at least
692 different compounds to accomplish that heretofore-
elusive goal.

Surprisingly, the aminopyridine worked, and the
resulting derivative—sulfapyridine—proved more potent
than sulfanilamide with wider-ranging antibacterial efficacy,
knocking out bacteria that cause pneumonia, meningitis,

gonorrhea, and a variety of other diseases. May & Baker began marketing sulfapyridine in 1938, and the sulfa drug was so popular and effective that during World War II, every American soldier carried a packet of sulfa powder in his first-aid kit.

VINYL

n 1838, French chemist Henri Victor Regnault exposed a glass flask filled with liquid vinyl chloride to light, inadvertently transforming the liquid compound into a white powder called polyvinyl chloride (better known as PVC or vinyl). For decades, no one could devise a practical way to use PVC for commercial purposes.

In 1926, Waldo L. Semon, a chemist at the B. F. Goodrich Company in Akron, Ohio, was searching for an adhesive that would bond rubber linings to metal industrial tanks. He polymerized vinyl chloride gas into a tough, resinous solid but found that this substance, when heated, was far too thick to work as an adhesive.

When he attempted to remove the PVC from the test tube, the test tube slipped from his hand and shattered on the floor. To Semon's surprise, the substance bounced. He kneaded it between his fingers, formed a small ball, and bounced it down the hallway.

Semon discovered that by mixing polyvinyl chloride powder with a solvent, he could mold the resulting rubbery gel into a stiff plastic material. But the waterproof, fire-resistant, and remarkably durable substance still would not bind to metal. After watching his wife, Marjorie, make curtains, Semon suggested that B. F. Goodrich coat fabrics with vinyl to produce waterproof material. The company used vinyl to make raincoats, umbrellas, shower curtains, waterproof linings, seals for shock absorbers, flexible tubing, suspenders, and wristwatch straps.

PVC has become the most widely used, inexpensive, versatile, and industrially important plastic material in the world—utilized for pipes, plastic wrap, drinking bottles, blister packaging, garden furniture, toys, credit cards, window frames, and much more.

ASPARTAME

In December 1965, James M. Schlatter, an organic chemist at G. D. Searle & Company in Skokie, Illinois, attempted to synthesize a drug to treat gastric ulcers. While heating crystallized aspartyl-phenylalanine methyl ester (aspartame) in a flask with methanol, Schlatter accidentally spilled some of the mixture onto the outside of the flask, which inadvertently got onto his fingers.

"At a slightly later stage, when licking my fingers to pick up a piece of paper, I noticed a very strong, sweet taste," recalled Schlatter in an affidavit. At first, he thought he had tasted sugar on his fingers from a doughnut he had eaten earlier in the day. Remembering that he had washed his hands before proceeding with his experiment, he traced the sweet-tasting substance on his fingers back to the flask of aspartame. Knowing that the human body safely metabolizes peptides like aspartame into their natural amino acids, Schlatter tasted the compound and confirmed that it was indeed the substance he had tasted on his fingers.

Searle executives commissioned a slew of safety studies on aspartame as a sweetener, obtained final approval from the U.S. Food and Drug Administration for aspartame as a food additive in 1981, and began marketing the sweetener that same year. Today, aspartame—found in NutraSweet, Equal, and thousands of food products—is the most popular artificial sweetener in the United States.

LASCAUX CAVE PAINTINGS

On September 12, 1940, four teenage boys—Marcel Ravidat, Jacques Marsal, Georges Agnel, and Simon Coencas—took a walk in the woods near the town of Montignac in southwestern France in search of a fabled tunnel that led to a treasure. As they walked through the woods, Ravidat's dog, Robot, ran ahead to explore a hole in the ground. The boys widened the hole, removed some rocks, crawled inside, and slid some fifty feet down a shaft into a chamber. Using oil lanterns to light the way, they followed a narrow passage that led to an underground cavern whose limestone walls and ceiling were covered with brilliantly colored paintings of animals.

When the boys began inviting friends and

charging admission, people from the village lined up to see the cave paintings. Overwhelmed by the number of visitors, the boys reported their finding to their schoolmaster, Leon Laval, who, after visiting the cave, telephoned French archaeologist Henri-Édouard-Prosper Breuil and instructed the boys to guard the cave from possible vandals. Upon visiting the cave, Breuil proclaimed the paintings authentically ancient.

Dubbed the "Sistine Chapel of Prehistoric Art," the main cavern of the Lascaux cave is decorated with approximately 600 painted and drawn animals and symbols and nearly 1,500 engravings dated to as early as 15,000 B.C.E. Considered among the finest examples of art by the Cro-Magnon people during the Upper Paleolithic period, the pictures depict horses, red deer, stags, bovines, felines, and what appear to be mythical creatures—all in astounding detail.

In 1963, France's minister of culture closed the cave to the public because carbon dioxide exhaled by thousands of visitors caused algae to grow and calcite to form over some of the paintings. A replica of the Lascaux cave was opened nearby in 1983 and receives tens of thousands of visitors annually.

IVORY SOAP

When Harley Procter decided in 1878 that the soap company founded by his father should develop a creamy white soap to compete with imported castile soaps, he asked his cousin, chemist James Gamble, to formulate the product. For decades, the Procter & Gamble

company claimed that one day after the soap went into production, a factory worker (who remains anonymous) forgot to switch off the master mixing machine when he went to lunch, accidentally whipping too much air into a batch of soap. Consumers were delighted by the floating soap and demanded more, and from then on, Procter & Gamble gave all its white soap an extra-long whipping. In 2004, however, company archivist Ed Rider discovered a notebook entry from 1863 in which Gamble wrote, "I made floating soap today. I think we'll make all our stock that way."

While the soap may not have originated by happenstance, the name did. Harley Procter, considering a long list of new names for his white soap, was inspired one Sunday morning in church when the pastor read Psalm 45: "All thy garments smell of myrrh, and aloes, and cassia, out of the ivory palaces, whereby they have made thee glad." A few years later, a chemist's analysis of Ivory soap indicated that 56/100 of the ingredients did not fall into the category of pure soap. Procter subtracted from 100, and wrote the slogan "99-44/100% Pure" which first appeared in Ivory's advertising in 1882. "It Floats" was added to Ivory's slogan in 1891.

AUSTIN MASTODONS

On December 30, 1984, Steve Tarkington, a backhoe operator excavating land to make way for the foundation of a twenty-two-story office building in Austin, Texas, unearthed a three-foot ivory tusk seventeen feet below street level.

"I just saw a piece of ivory flashing in the bucket," Tarkington told the Asso-ciated Press. "I just threw it out and looked at it later."

Archaeologist Alton Briggs, employed by the contractor to be on hand during the excavation, identified the tusk as belonging to a mastodon, a prehistoric animal related to the elephant. Briggs subsequently unearthed tusks of three mastodons, spinal bones, and teeth. The bones, found in gray clay, were lying in what may have been a watering hole approximately 15,000 years ago. The Austin pit ranks as the second-largest repository of mastodon bones in North America, behind a mastodon site in Missouri.

MR. COFFEE MACHINE

n the 1960s, Vince Marotta presided over North American Systems in Pepper Pike, Ohio, building shopping malls and housing developments. When business slowed in 1968, Marotta fell ill, and while recuperating in bed, he realized how fed up he was with his wife's percolated coffee and decided to develop a better way to make coffee. He contacted the Pan American Coffee Bureau and discovered that South American coffee growers believed that the best way to extract the oil from coffee beans was to pour water, heated to 200 degrees Fahrenheit, over the ground beans.

Marotta hired engineers Erwin Schulze and Edward Able to devise a bimetal actuator to control the temperature of the water. Observing how restaurants used a white cloth in their large coffee percolators to capture loose grounds and eliminate sediment, Marotta decided to use a paper filter in his coffee maker. He paid a paper company to cut and flue the filters from an existing paper stock. Determined to give his coffeemaker a simple, catchy name, Marotta came up with "Mr. Coffee" off the top of his head.

Marotta showed up at the 1970 Housewares Convention in Chicago with a prototype for the Mr. Coffee machine. On the spot, he hired Bill Howe, a buyer with Hamilton Beach, to represent his product. Howe invited 100 buyers up to Marotta's hotel room for coffee, and, within two years, Mr. Coffee was selling 42,000 coffee machines a day. Mr. Coffee became the best-selling coffeemaker in the world, and Marotta sold the company in 1987.

X-RAYS

On the evening of November 8, 1895, German physicist Wilhelm Konrad Röntgen, director of the Physical Institute of the University of Würzburg, decided to discharge electricity at high voltage through a gas in an evacuated glass tube to see if he could detect the emission of cathode rays with a fluorescent detecting screen. Convinced that the strong phosphorescence of the 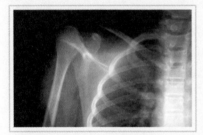 cathode tube obscured the weak fluorescence of the detecting screen, Röntgen covered the glass tube with a thick black carton to seal off all emitted light. He darkened the room and turned on the high voltage generator to make sure no phosphorescent light escaped from the black carton. It did not.

Röntgen was about to turn off the generator and turn on the room lights when he suddenly noticed a weak light shimmering a few feet away from the black carton. At first he thought a mirror in the room was reflecting a small beam of light escaping from a tiny hole in the black carton. But there was no mirror in the room. Röntgen lit a match and discovered, much to his surprise, that the source of the light was the small fluorescent screen lying on a bench.

Since cathode rays could not light up a fluorescent screen placed more than two or three inches away from the tube, Röntgen realized that he had encountered a new form of radiation that had penetrated the box. He observed that these mysterious "X-rays" penetrated various objects and lit up the fluorescent screen to different degrees, depending upon the density of the object. He instructed his wife Anna to hold her hand in the path of the rays against a photographic plate. When Röntgen developed the plate, he discovered an image of his wife's hand that showed the shadows of her bones and a ring she wore, surrounded by the penumbra of her flesh. Röntgen had created the first X-ray image, and shortly thereafter, hospitals throughout the world were using X-rays to help diagnose patients.

STAINLESS STEEL

I n 1912, British metallurgist Harry Brearley, head of the Brown Firth Research Laboratory in Sheffield, England, was researching ways to eliminate erosion in gun barrels caused by the friction of the fired bullets. Needing a harder metal that could resist higher

temperatures, Brearley spent months experimenting with various steel alloys, none of which reduced barrel erosion significantly. He tossed the failed samples into a junk pile.

Months later, on August 13, 1913, Brearley noticed that one of the failed samples in the junk pile had remained shiny and bright while the others had rusted. That alloy, Brearley realized, contained 12.8 percent chromium and 0.24 percent carbon, accounting for its resistance to erosion. Discovering that this new steel strongly resisted chemical attack from vinegar and lemon juice, Brearley recognized that his "rustless steel" could revolutionize the cutlery industry. He had a set of knives made at a local cutler's, R. F. Mosley, where cutlery manager Ernest Stuart dubbed the new metal "stainless steel."

EGGS BENEDICT

One morning in 1894, dapper New York City stockbroker Lemuel Benedict, suffering from a hangover, wandered into the Waldorf Hotel at Fifth Avenue and 33rd Street and ordered two poached eggs, bacon, buttered toast, and a small pitcher of hollandaise sauce. He placed the eggs and bacon on top of each slice of toast and topped them with hollandaise sauce.

Oscar Tschirky, the widely known maître d'hôtel at the Waldorf, noticed Benedict's innovation and tested it for himself. He substituted Canadian ham for the bacon and an open-faced English muffin for the toast and added the new item to the menu as eggs Benedict, in honor of his creative customer.

"Lemuel Benedict reveled in the attention and prestige that resulted from his breakfast order," reported the *New York Times* in 2007. "But his original request had specified toast, and he never warmed to the idea of English muffins."

The eminence of the Waldorf Hotel established eggs Benedict as a classic American dish, and in 1931, when the hotel, renamed the Waldorf-Astoria, moved to Park Avenue, eggs Benedict had become a distinctive feature of the hotel. In 1972, McDonald's franchisee Herb Peterson created the Egg McMuffin based on eggs Benedict.

SILLY PUTTY

n 1943, the United States War Production Board asked General Electric to synthesize a cheap substitute for rubber. James Wright, a company engineer assigned to the project in New Haven, Connecticut, combined boric acid and silicone oil, developing a pliant compound dubbed "nutty putty" that appeared to have no real commercial use.

In 1949, Peter Hodgson, a former advertising copywriter writing the catalog for a New Haven toy store, happened to witness a demonstration of the "nutty putty" at a party. He bought twenty-one pounds of the putty for $147, hired a Yale student to separate it into half-ounce balls, and marketed the putty inside colored plastic eggs

as Silly Putty, a name he came up with while playing with the pink polymer.

When Silly Putty outsold every other item in the toy store catalog (second only to a fifty-cent box of Crayola crayons), Hodgson mass-produced Silly Putty as "the toy with one moving part," selling up to three hundred eggs a day. In August 1950, the *New Yorker* featured a short piece on Silly Putty in "Talk of the Town," launching an overnight novelty. Silly Putty was originally shipped in egg cartons purchased from the Connecticut Cooperative Poultry Association. In 1977, Crayola acquired the exclusive manufacturing rights to Silly Putty.

MACHU PICCHU

On July 24, 1911, Yale University professor Hiram Bingham, following the Urubamba River in Peru to search for the lost Inca capital of Vilcabamba in the Andes Mountains, paid a local farmer named Melchor Arteaga to lead him to a nearby ruin. Arteaga led the explorer 2,000 feet up a precipitous slope to a grass hut, where an 11-year-old Quechua boy, Pablito Alvarez, took him the rest of the way to the jungle-covered ruins of the "lost" city of Machu Picchu, whose

existence was known to Quechua peasants who farmed the area. Bingham believed he had discovered Vilcabamba, but archaeologists have shown that Machu Picchu was one of a series of personal royal estates built by an Inca emperor along the Inca trail.

Built around 1460, Machu Picchu seems to have been abandoned after the Spanish conquest of Peru in 1572, even though the conquistadors never found it. Bingham began to excavate the site immediately, erroneously called the complex "The Lost City of the Incas," and brought Machu Picchu to worldwide attention. Believed to have been a palace complex of the fifteenth century Inca emperor Pachacuti, Machu Picchu means "old mountain" in the Quechua language.

S.O.S STEEL WOOL PADS

n 1917, Edwin Cox, a struggling door-to-door aluminum cookware salesman in San Francisco, sought a gimmick to help boost his floundering business. In his kitchen, he developed a steel wool scouring pad caked with dried soap as a free gift to housewives to get himself invited inside their homes to demonstrate his wares. A few months later, demand for the soap-encrusted pads snowballed, prompting Cox to quit the aluminum cookware business and go to work for himself.

Mrs. Edwin Cox, the inventor's wife, named the soap pads S.O.S., for "Save Our Saucepans," convinced that she had cleverly adapted the Morse code international

distress signal for "Save Our Ships." In fact, the distress signal S.O.S. doesn't stand for anything. It's simply a combination of three letters represented by three identical marks (the *S* is three dots; the *O* is three dashes). Cox deleted the period after the last *S* in the brand name to obtain a trademark for what would otherwise be an international distress symbol.

BAKELITE

n 1907, Belgian immigrant Leo Hendrik Baekeland, a former organic chemistry professor at the University of Ghent, attempted to synthesize a substitute for shellac in his home laboratory in Yonkers, New York. At the time, shellac was made from shells of the lac beetle (explaining the origin of the word *shellac*).

Combining formaldehyde and phenol, Baekeland noticed that under certain conditions, the mixture produced a resin that was apparently insoluble. He realized that if he could find a solvent that would dissolve

the worthless resin he might produce a varnish superior to shellac. But Baekeland could not find such a solvent.

He did discover that mixing and warming equal parts of formaldehyde and phenol in the presence of an alkali caused the solution to separate into two layers: an upper watery substance and a lower resin that was soft, pliable, and soluble in alcohol. When heated under pressure, the shaped resin baked into a rock-solid, insoluble plastic—resisting heat, acids, and electrical currents. Baekeland called his discovery Bakelite, received a patent for his process, and became known as the "father of plastics."

Unlike rubber, which dried out and cracked, Bakelite endured, making the perfect synthetic polymer from which to mold bracelets, pot and pan handles, the heads of electrical plugs, radio dials, bowling balls, radiator caps, and telephones—tinted in a variety of colors.

GRAVITY

In 1665, when the University of Cambridge in England closed to prevent the spread of the plague, which had broken out in London, recent graduate Isaac Newton returned home to Woolsthrope-by-Colsterworth, a hamlet in Lincolnshire, England.

One day during the two years he spent at home in study and reflection, the 23-year-old Newton sat in contemplation in the orchard when an apple happened to fall from a tree. His mind fueled by his Cambridge education, Newton questioned why apples always fell perpendicular to the ground and toward the earth's center, rather than sideways or upward. He reasoned that the earth drew the apple toward it, and this drawing power resided at the earth's center. He further surmised that if matter

attracts matter, it does so in proportion to its mass. In other words, just as the earth attracts the apple, the apple attracts the earth. He called this force gravity.

Newton extrapolated that the same gravity that governed the earth and the apple also governed the earth and the moon. Based on this notion, he calculated the force necessary to hold the moon in its orbit. He pictured the moon like a stone thrown horizontally, always falling to earth, but never reaching the ground due to the curvature of the earth and the velocity of the moon. In 1687, more than twenty years after first contemplating the apple falling from a tree, Newton published his theory of gravitation in his three-volume book *The Principia*— revolutionizing physics.

LEA & PERRINS®
WORCESTERSHIRE SAUCE

n 1835, when nobleman Lord Marcus Sandys, governor of Bengal, India, retired to his home in Ombersley, England, he longed for his favorite Indian sauce. He took the recipe to a drugstore on Broad Street in nearby Worcester where he commissioned the shopkeepers, John Lea and William Perrins, to mix up a batch.

Lea and Perrins prepared a few extra gallons of the sauce in the hope of selling the excess to other customers, but they found the taste revolting. They stored jars of the pungent fishy concoction in the cellar where they sat undisturbed until Lea and Perrins rediscovered them two years later when housecleaning.

Upon tasting the aged sauce, Lea and Perrins were amazed to discover that the aged concoction now tasted wonderful.

They began bottling the sauce as a local dip, and through word of mouth, Worcestershire sauce (named after the county of its origin) was soon being used across the British Isles.

When Lea and Perrins' salesmen convinced British passenger ships to put the sauce on their dining room tables, Worcestershire sauce became an established steak sauce across Europe and the United States.

GUNPOWDER AND FIREWORKS

Around 808 C.E., a Chinese alchemist, attempting to create an elixir of eternal life, heated sulfur and charcoal together and then added saltpeter (potassium nitrate), a powerful oxidizing agent used in medical compounds. The mixture exploded with a flash and a loud bang.

The Tang dynasty book *Classified Essentials of the Mysterious Tao of the True Origins of Things*, written in the mid-ninth century, warns against mixing an elixir from similar ingredients: "Some have heated together sulfur, realgar (arsenic disulphide), and saltpeter with honey; smoke and flames result, so that their hands and faces have been burnt, and even the whole house where they were working burnt down."

Before long, Chinese alchemists discovered that when packed into a bamboo tube and ignited, the mixture rocketed skyward and exploded, lighting up the sky with fireworks. By 919 C.E., military commanders realized that this exploding powder could also be used to make weapons. They filled a papier-mâché ball with the powder and, after lighting a gunpowder fuse, used a catapult to hurl the ball at the enemy.

By 1116 C.E., the Chinese had invented the canon to fire metal "thunder-crash bombs" filled with gunpowder, sending shrapnel flying when the ball exploded. The Chinese also developed rocket-powdered flaming arrows, flamethrowers (tubes filled with petroleum distillates and ignited with a gunpowder fuse), and the first gun—revolutionizing warfare and forever changing military strategy. The Chinese managed to keep the recipe for gunpowder secret until the thirteenth century, when Arabs and Europeans figured out the formula.

POPCORN

Around 80,000 B.C.E., cave men and women in prehistoric America placed maize kernels too close to the fire, accidentally creating popcorn. For hundreds of years before the arrival of Europeans, Native Americans grew maize, a grain indigenous to North and South America, and used popcorn for food and decoration in religious ceremonies. In 1492, Italian explorer Christopher Columbus noted in his journal that the Native Americans in the West Indies wore popcorn corsages, headbands, and necklaces. In 1620, Native Americans in Massachusetts brought bowlfuls of popcorn to the first Thanksgiving feast with the

Pilgrims. In 1700, women from Boston to the Carolinas made breakfast cereal by pouring milk and sugar over popcorn.

Charles Cretors of Chicago, Illinois, invented the first popcorn machine in 1885—an enormous, cumbersome cart with a gasoline burner. Street vendors were soon pushing steam- or gas-powered popcorn machines through fairs, parks, and expositions—following crowds. To this day, the Cretors family manufactures most of the popcorn machines operating at movie theaters and fairs.

The United States grows most of the popcorn kernels consumed in the world, and the average American eats fifty-two quarts of popcorn in a year—more than the citizens of any other country. Nebraska and Indiana lead the states in popcorn kernel production.

ÖTZI THE ICEMAN

On September 19, 1991, Erika and Helmut Simon of Nuremberg, Germany, were hiking in the Ötztal Alps in South Tyrol, Italy. Descending from the Finail peak near the Hauslabjoch Pass, the couple decided to take a shortcut and left the marked footpath. At an altitude of 10,498 feet above sea level, they noticed some rubbish in a rocky gully filled with melting snow and ice from a glacier. On closer inspection, they realized the rubbish was actually a decaying human corpse jutting out of the water. The Simons took a photograph of what they believed to be the long-lost victim of a mountaineering accident and contacted the authorities.

Three days later, forensic experts freed the body from the ice and brought the corpse, along with pieces of leather and hide, to the Institute of Forensic Medicine in Innsbruck, Austria. Archaeologist Konrad Spindler, professor of ancient and early history at the University of Innsbruck, dated the whole find to be "at least four thousand years old," making the Neolithic man, who had been buried in the glacier and essentially freeze-dried along with much of his clothing and possessions, one of the oldest mummies in the world and one of the best-preserved ancient humans. Carbon-14 dating proved that the iceman lived between 3350 and 3100 B.C.E., during the Bronze Age, and studies at the University of Innsbruck revealed that he died at approximately forty-six years of age. Viennese reporter Karl Wendl gave the iceman the name "Ötzi" in reference to the adjoining Ötz Valley where the mummy was found.

Ötzi the Iceman, along with his clothing (sewn from skins of mountain goat and antelope and insulated with hay) and tools (an ax, a dagger, a longbow, arrows, and a tinder kit for making fires) can be viewed at the South Tyrol Museum of Archaeology in Bolzano, Italy.

GREEN GIANT

I n 1925, the Minnesota Valley Canning Company in Le Sueur, Minnesota began selling cans of an unusually large green pea bred to be more flavorful, more tender, and sweeter than previously sold peas—giving birth to the name Green Giant to describe the new peas. The company's trademark attorney, Warwick Keegin, insisting that the descriptive name could not be trademarked, suggested adding a picture of a giant to the label so the name— referring to the giant, not the peas—could be trademarked.

A drawing of a wild-haired, non-green giant wearing an animal skin helped the company secure a trademark for the brand name and first appeared in advertising in 1928. Keegin later argued for a truly green giant, and in 1935, Leo Burnett, a young, aspiring Chicago advertising man, revised the giant—adding green skin, a leaf cloak, and a smile. The Jolly Green Giant lives in the Valley of the Jolly Green Giant and shouts his catchphrase, "Ho, Ho, Ho!"

The Minnesota Valley Canning Company soon had six canneries in Minnesota, marketing a wide variety of vegetables, and the Green Giant came to symbolize the entire company, not merely the large pea. In 1950, the Minnesota Valley Canning Company changed its name to Green Giant Company, which, in 1972, introduced Sprout—a walking, talking Brussels sprout—as the Green Giant's sidekick.

OXYGEN

Eighteenth-century English chemist Joseph Priestley believed that anything that could burn contained a special substance called phlogiston. When the object was burned, phlogiston escaped into the atmosphere. Priestley used a "burning lens," a large magnifying glass he received as a gift, to focus sunlight to heat substances to high temperatures.

In 1774, Priestley heated red oxide of mercury and red oxide of lead, and captured the resulting gas in a glass vessel. He happened to have a lit candle sitting nearby, so he placed the candle inside the glass vessel and discovered, much to his surprise, that the gas did not extinguish the

flame. Instead, he observed that the candle "burned in this air with a remarkably vigorous flame," a reaction he could not explain, according to his book, *Experiments and Observations on Different Kinds of Air*. Priestley also discovered that a mouse would stay conscious twice as long in a sealed container of the gas as it would in a sealed container of air. The scientist inhaled the gas and felt remarkably refreshed. He called this new gas "dephlogistonated air."

Two months later, French chemist Antoine Laurent Lavoisier repeated Priestley's experiment and discovered that the resulting gas was a component of air. Erroneously convinced that his newly discovered element was the active ingredient contained in all acids, Lavoisier named the gas *oxygen* (Greek for "acid maker"). The discovery of oxygen also enabled Lavoisier to debunk Priestley's phlogiston theory. Combustion did not result from the combination of phlogiston and dephlogistonated air, as Priestley insisted, but rather from the combination of oxygen with other substances.

DIXIE CUPS

n 1908, Hugh Moore worked for the American Water Supply Company of New York to market a vending machine that for one penny would dispense a cool drink of water in an individual, clean, disposable paper cup. Moore soon realized that his sanitary cups had greater sales potential than his water, particularly when Dr. Samuel Crumbine, a health official in Dodge City, Kansas, began crusading for a law to ban the public tin dipper—a communal cup welded to a long handle.

Lacking the funds to manufacture enough paper cups to abolish the tin dipper, Moore and his associate, Lawrence Luellen, moved into the Waldorf-Astoria Hotel, and with a few handmade samples, persuaded investors to pump $200,000 into the venture. That same year, Kansas passed the first state law abolishing the public dipper, and Professor Alvin Davison of Lafayette College published a study on the germs present on public dipping tins in schools.

As state after state outlawed public drinking tins, Moore and his associates created a paper cup dispenser to be distributed for free to businesses and schools that would then buy the paper cups.

Moore's paper cup factory was located next door to the Dixie Doll Company in the same building in New York City. The word *Dixie* printed on the company's door reminded Moore of the story he had heard as a boy about "dixies," the ten-dollar bank notes printed with the French word *dix* in big letters across the face of the bill by a New Orleans bank renowned for its strong currency in the early 1800s. The "dixies," Moore decided, had the qualities he wanted people to associate with his paper cups.

WESTERN HEMISPHERE

talian explorer Christopher Columbus thought that when he crossed the Atlantic Ocean in 1492, he would land in Asia. He had no idea that a landmass existed between the two continents and, after four trips, remained convinced that he had landed in Asia—not the New World. Columbus miscalculated the circumference of the globe by 7,600 miles and inaccurately estimated the earth to be 25 percent smaller than it actually is. He also estimated Asia to be larger and the Atlantic Ocean to be smaller than they really are.

Unbeknownst to Columbus, he actually landed on the Bahamian island of San Salvador (which he believed to be an island of the Indies), Cuba (which he thought to be a part of China), and the Hispaniola (which he insisted was the Far East). He named the islands the West Indies (because he incorrectly thought they were part of the Indies islands of Asia) and dubbed the natives "Indians" (wrongly convinced he was in India). On his third journey, Columbus set foot on the South American coast in Venezuela, convinced that he had discovered a new continent southeast of China.

In 1501, Italian explorer and cartographer Amerigo Vespucci discovered present-day Rio de Janeiro. He realized that Brazil and the West Indies were part of a new continent in a western hemisphere located between Europe and Asia, which he called the New World. Columbus died in 1506, still clinging to the misbegotten belief that he had reached Asia.

DEAD SEA SCROLLS

n March 1947, fourteen-year-old Bedouin shepherd Mohammed Dib went searching for a goat that had strayed into the barren cliffs near Qumran on the northwest coast of the Dead Sea. He discovered a small opening in one of the cliffs, tossed a stone into it, and heard the shattering of pottery inside the cave. Frightened by the sound, he ran away.

Mohammed returned with a friend and the duo crawled inside the cave where they found several large earthen jars containing aged scrolls of parchment wrapped in linen. The boys brought three scrolls back to their camp, and, after showing them to antiquities dealers in Bethlehem, Mohammed showed

the scrolls to Khalil Eskander Shahin, a Syrian Orthodox merchant and cobbler. Shahin brought the scrolls to the attention of Mar Athanasius Yeshua Samuel, the Syrian Orthodox archbishop at St. Mark's Monastery in the Old City of Jerusalem.

Realizing the scrolls might be valuable finds, the archbishop purchased the scrolls from Mohammed for one hundred dollars and sent them to the American School of Oriental Research in Jerusalem for examination. There, Drs. John C. Trever and William Brownlee recognized the archaic forms of the Hebrew letters written on the scrolls and identified the biblical book of Isaiah, a rule book for a community, and a commentary on the biblical book of the prophet Habakkuk. They sent photographs of one scroll to Dr. William F. Albright, an expert on Hebrew paleography at the Johns Hopkins University in Baltimore, Maryland, who dated the manuscript to roughly 100 B.C.E. (later confirmed by carbon-14 dating), making the scrolls the oldest Biblical manuscripts yet discovered.

MARILYN MONROE

When her husband joined the U.S. Merchant Marine in 1944 during World War II, nineteen-year-old Norma Jeane Dougherty went to work alongside her mother-in-law at the Radioplane Company, a defense plant in Van Nuys, California. After working as a parachute inspector, she was promoted to spray plane fuselages with liquid plastic. "I worked in overalls and kept my head covered most of the time so that the dope wouldn't get into my hair, since it was messy and difficult to wash out," she recalled in *Marilyn: Her Life in Her Own Words*.

One day, U.S. Army photographer David Conover, assigned to take publicity shots of pretty women working in defense plants to be published in magazines and newspapers to boost morale, noticed Dougherty working. "First he took pictures of me in my overalls, but when he discovered I had a sweater in my locker, he asked if I would mind wearing it for more pictures." Those photos appeared in hundreds of army camp newspapers, including *Stars and Stripes* and *Yank* magazine.

A few weeks later, Conover showed the pictures to commercial photographer Potter Hueth, who invited Dougherty to model for him. Hueth showed his pictures of Dougherty to Emmeline Snively, the head of the Blue Book Modeling Agency. Snively arranged to have Dougherty trained and sent on assignments, turning her into one of the most popular magazine cover girls. At Snively's urging, Dougherty dyed her hair blonde, and shortly after talent scout Ben Lyon helped her land a movie contract with Twentieth Century Fox, Dougherty changed her name. Lyon suggested the first name Marilyn, and Dougherty added her grandmother's surname—Monroe.

SMART DUST

I n 2002, while Jamie Link conducted her doctoral work in chemistry and biochemistry at the University of California, San Diego, one of the silicon chips she was working on burst and crumbled into a bunch of tiny pieces. With help from professor Michael Sailor, Link soon discovered that the minute fragments still functioned

as sensors, resulting in the first self-assembling, programmable silcon particles.

Nicknamed "smart dust," each millimeter-sized particle is a mirrored surface that can stick to a desired target and change color to signal what it has found. Link and Sailor used electrochemical corrosion techniques to engineer the particles with a different color on each side. One side sticks to the target and the other side reports information to the viewer. For instance, in the presence of a chemical toxin in sewage water, or a harmful gas in a room, the green side of the smart dust attaches to the pollutant and the red side becomes visible to the naked eye. The smart dust has theoretical applications for environmental testing, biological agent detection, medical diagnostics and research, tumor treatment, drug delivery, and many other commercial, medical, and scientific purposes.

DOUGHNUTS

egend holds that in 1847, sea captain Hanson Crockett Gregory of Rockport, Maine, was eating a small, deep-fried cake while steering his ship when he encountered rough waters. Needing two hands to steer the ship, Gregory impaled the pastry on a spoke of the steering wheel, inadvertently poking out the soggy center. From then on, Gregory ordered his cook to make the doughnuts with a hole in the center. That legend seems to have originated in the 1946 children's book *Cap'n Dow and the Hole in the Doughnut* by Le Grand Henderson.

Hanson Crockett Gregory told a different story. While sailing aboard a lime ship at age sixteen in 1847, Gregory did indeed snack on small, deep-fried cakes. Those cakes would be fried around

the edges, but the center would remain uncooked dough—causing indigestion. Realizing that a hole in the center of the cake would solve the problem, Gregory removed the cover from the ship's tin pepperbox and used it to punch a hole in the middle of the cake—leaving a properly fried doughnut.

Upon returning home to Camden, Maine, Gregory found his mother making doughnuts in the kitchen and offered to make some for her with a hole in the center. "So I made her one or two and then showed her how," Gregory told the *Washington Post* in 1916. "She then made several panfuls and sent them down to Rockland, just outside Camden. Everybody was delighted, and they never made doughnuts any other way except the way I showed my mother." And that's the hole story.

URANUS

On March 13, 1781, British astronomer William Herschel, using a homemade telescope to survey all the stars too faint to see with the human eye, suddenly noticed an object that, over time, moved in front of the star background. Herschel quickly surmised that this celestial body was orbiting the sun and that it was a new planet—the first discovered since ancient times.

German astronomer Johann Elert Bode realized that astronomers had unwittingly observed Uranus as far back as 1690, mistaking it for a star.

Herschel proposed to name the new planet after King George III, but Bode, having determined the orbit of

Uranus, urged that scientists follow the convention of naming planets for the Roman gods and suggested the name Uranus—possibly because Uranus was the father of Saturn who was the father of Jupiter.

In 1977, astronomers using the Kuiper Airborne Observatory to watch a bright star pass behind Uranus—providing a glimpse of the planet's atmosphere—saw the star suddenly blink out nine times. They realized that they had accidentally discovered nine rings around Uranus that successively blocked the light of the star.

ETCH A SKETCH

One day in the late 1950s, French electrician André Cassagnes was installing a light-switch plate at the factory where he worked. The factory manufactured Lincrusta, a molded wall covering made to imitate bas-relief. When Cassagnes peeled the translucent protective decal off the new switch plate, he accidentally

made some pencil marks on it. He noticed that the marks were visible on the reverse side of the decal. Some aluminum powder, charged with static electricity, had clung to the decal. The pencil had scraped off some of the powder, inadvertently creating visible lines.

Over the next few years, Cassagnes developed a rectangular grey screen framed by a thin red box filled with fine aluminum powder, which electrostatically adhered to the underside of the screen. A joystick controlled the movement of a stylus hidden beneath the screen, which then scraped off the powder, creating a line on the screen as if by magic. Shaking the toy erased the image, recoating the screen with aluminum and allowing the user to start over from scratch. Cassagnes named the toy *L'Écran Magique* (French for "Magic Screen").

Cassagnes introduced the toy at the 1959 Nuremberg Toy Fair. The Ohio Art Company bought the rights for $25,000 and changed the name to Etch A Sketch. Cassagnes worked with the company's chief engineer, Jerry Burger, changing the joystick to two white knobs—the left to control the horizontal movement of the stylus, the right to control the vertical movement—to mimic a television set. First marketed in 1960, Etch A Sketch became the best-selling toy of that holiday season. Eventually advertised as "the world's first laptop," Etch A Sketch sold more than 150 million units of various models by the time Cassagnes died at age 86 in 2013.

HERCULANEUM

n 1709, while digging a well in the Italian town of Resina, just outside of Naples, workers discovered fragments of precious marble statues and mosaics. Two years later, Prince d'Elbeuf, a general in the Austrian army, built a palace in the nearby town of Portici, which he wished to embellish with rare marbles. Learning of the well in Resina, he bought the land and secured permission from the Austrian government (which controlled the kingdom of Naples) to excavate the property and keep whatever he found.

D'Elbeuf's men dug down ninety feet into the theater of ancient Herculaneum, the Roman town buried under lava and ash since the eruption of Mount Vesuvius in 79 C.E.

For five years, he plundered a vast number of bronze, marble, and terracotta antiquities without ever knowing the name or the history of the site.

Ultimately, the Austrian viceroy intervened, confiscated all the statues and artifacts, and sent them to Vienna and Dresden. In 1737, Charles III of Spain drove out the Austrians and assumed the throne of Naples. He built a palace at Portici and wishing to decorate it with relics, chose a Spanish colonel, Roque Joachim de Alcubierre, to resume the excavations beneath Resina. The following year, workers discovered fragments of a bronze horse, statues of three Roman consuls, and an inscription identifying the Theatre of Herculaneum, at last confirming that Resina and Portici sat above the long-buried city of Herculaneum. De Alcubierre's crude and merciless excavation methods, however, caused untold destruction of the virtually pristine Herculaneum. In 1750, the king appointed Swiss architect Karl Weber to the excavation team. Weber's systematic methods helped preserve the lost city, including the Villa of the Papyri, described by archaeologist Amedeo Maiuri as "the most valuable and richest villa of the ancient world."

POMPEII

n 1594, architect Domenico Fontana hired workmen to dig a tunnel south of Naples, Italy, to divert the waters of the River Foce (to provide water for an armaments factory at Torre Annunziata). While digging the tunnel, the workmen uncovered slabs of marble, frescoed walls, and statues with inscriptions in vernacular Latin. At the time, no one identified the ancient site.

Nearly a century later, in 1689, a farmer digging a well in that same area found an inscription that referred to

a town councilor of Pompeii. Neapolitan architect Francesco Pichetti insisted that the inscription meant that the site was the villa of a Pompeian councilor, not the lost city of Pompeii, which had been destroyed by the eruption of Mount Vesuvius on August 24 in the year 79 C.E.

In 1748, Col. Roque Joachim de Alcubierre, who had excavated and caused countless damage to the ruins at Herculaneum under the command of the Bourbon king of Naples, Charles III, turned his attention further south to the channel dug by Domenico Fontana, where he might unearth more relics to fill Charles's Royal Museum in the palace at Portici. Fortunately, pockets of lethal carbon monoxide gas trapped in the rocks impeded de Alcubierre's endeavors at Pompeii, and he went back to Herculaneum.

De Alcubierre later returned to Pompeii with Swiss architect Karl Weber, and working together in 1755, the two men found the well-preserved Praedia of Julia Felix (a large townhouse). Ultimately, an inscription found in 1763 reading *respublica Pompeianorum* ("the commonwealth of the Pompeians") positively identified the ruins as the fabled city of Pompeii.

PHOSPHORUS

I n 1669, German alchemist Hennig Brand, working in Hamburg, attempted to make gold by letting a jar of human urine stand for several days to putrefy. Convinced that the yellow color of urine indicated that it contained gold, he boiled the rotting liquid down to a paste, heated the resulting paste, and drew the vapors into water. Instead of condensing to gold, as Brand anticipated, the drawn vapors produced a white, waxy substance that glowed in the dark. He named  his accidental discovery *phosphorus* (Greek for "light bearer"), marking the first time anyone had discovered an element unknown to ancient peoples.

Brand's accidental discovery would ultimately prove to be more valuable than gold when inventors used it to create fire on demand—by rubbing phosphorus and sulfur together. Brand tried to keep his method of producing phosphorus secret in the hopes of selling the process.

In 1678, German chemist Johann Kunckel, unable to convince Brand to share his secret, independently devised a process to produce the element. Brand did share the secret with his friend, Dr. Johann Daniel Krafft, who, seeking a buyer for Brand, demonstrated the new wonder substance in the courts of Europe, during which time English scientist Robert Boyle witnessed the presentation. Krafft published his technique for producing phosphorus in 1679, and the following year, Boyle developed his own method to make phosphorus from urine, improving on Brand's process by adding sand, and published his technique in 1682.

WHISTLING TEAKETTLE

n 1921, Joseph Block, a retired cookware executive from New York, toured the Gebruder Hansel teakettle factory in Westphalia, Germany. Seeing so many teakettles at once suddenly triggered a childhood memory in Block's mind. He remembered watching his father design a pressurized potato cooker that emitted a whistling sound when the cooking cycle finished. Block urged the teakettle manufacturer to create a teakettle that whistled when the water boiled. The simple idea of combining a teakettle with a whistle intrigued the factory owner, who immediately

 produced thirty-six whistling teakettles, put them on sale at Wertheim's department store in Berlin, and sold out in less than three hours.

The following year, Block came out of retirement to debut his whistling teakettle in the United States at a Chicago housewares fair. He kept at least one kettle whistling throughout the weeklong show, prompting bewitched store buyers to place huge orders for the one-dollar item. Before long, Block was selling 35,000 whistling teakettles a month to department stores across the United States.

KOTEX

n 1914, Kimberly-Clark & Company in Neenah, Wisconsin, developed Cellucotton, a cotton substitute made from cellulose wadding and used by the U.S. Army as surgical padding during World War I. In army hospitals and first-aid stations, resourceful nurses adapted the highly absorbent Cellucotton pads for use as disposable sanitary napkins. Word got back to the executives at Kimberly-

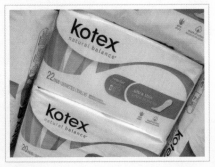

Clark, and in 1920, the company repackaged Cellucotton as Kotex (a combination of the words *cotton* and *texture*), introducing its first consumer product and the world's first disposable feminine hygiene product.

Because most Americans considered the product improper, Kimberly-Clark decided to protect its pristine image by creating a separate entity, the Cellucotton Products Company, to market Kotex. Although many stores refused to carry the product and many magazines declined to run advertisements for it, the company persisted and sanitary napkins gradually gained acceptance. Finally, in 1926, Montgomery Ward advertised Kotex in its catalog.

To help women avoid the embarrassment of asking a drugstore clerk for a box of Kotex stored on a shelf behind the counter, Kimberly-Clark urged storeowners to display the product on countertops so customers could quietly take a pack and drop their money in a box. By 1927, sales of Kotex exceeded $11 million and the product was sold in 57 countries.

THE CALENDAR

Around 738 B.C.E., Romulus, the first emperor of Rome, instituted a calendar that contained only 304 days for a total of ten months: Martius, Aprilis, Maius, Junius, Quintilis, Sextilis, September, October, November, and December. The prefixes of the last six months were taken from the Roman words for five, six, seven, eight, nine, and ten.

The months of the calendar quickly slid out of alignment with the 365-day year. To correct this, the second Roman emperor, Numa Pompilius, added two more months to the calendar (January at the beginning of the calendar and February at the end of the calendar). In 452 B.C.E., the Decemvirs—a commission of ten Roman magistrates—changed the order of the months, putting January first and February second.

In 46 B.C.E., Roman emperor Julius Caesar moved New Year's Day from March I to January I. Centuries later the Romans changed the name of the month of Quintilis to July (in memory of Julius Caesar) and the name of Sextilis to August (in memory of Caesar Augustus). To this day, September (with the Roman prefix for seven) is the ninth month of the calendar, October (with the prefix for eight) is the tenth month, November (with the prefix for nine) is the eleventh month, and December (with the prefix for ten) is the twelfth month.

BLUE JEANS

I n 1871, Latvian immigrant Jacob Davis, a tailor in Reno, Nevada, had a brawny customer who kept ripping the pockets and seams of the pants that Davis made for him. Determined to devise a way to reinforce the man's denim trousers, Davis decided to put copper rivets at the points susceptible to the most strain—the corners of pockets and the base of the button fly.

When the riveted pants became an instant hit with his customers, Davis decided to apply for a patent to safeguard his innovative process. Not having the $68 required to file the papers, he decided to seek a business partner and thought of Jewish-German immigrant Levi Strauss, the dry goods wholesaler in San Francisco from whom he purchased bolts of denim cloth.

In 1872, Davis wrote a letter to Strauss, proposing that Strauss pay for the paperwork and that they hold the patent together. Strauss agreed. The two men received a patent on May 20, 1873, the day now considered the official birthday of blue jeans. Strauss hired Davis to oversee production of the riveted pants at his San Francisco plant, and the Levi Strauss & Co. marketed the first riveted clothing later that year. Shortly afterward, workingmen of all trades were purchasing the riveted denim pants and extolling their unparalleled sturdiness.

The patent gave Levi Strauss & Co. the exclusive right to make riveted clothing for nearly twenty years, cornering the market without any competition.

LINOLEUM

I n 1860, Fredrick Walton, a 26-year-old rubber manufacturer working for his father in Haughton Green, England, looked into a leftover paint can and discovered that a tough, thick skin of oxidized linseed oil had formed over the paint. Determined to come up

with a use for this tough skin, Walton moved to Chiswick, near London and, after some experimentation, discovered that alcohol dissolved a sample of oxidized linseed oil removed from a can of paint. He combined the resulting varnish with ground cork and color pigments and pressed the mixture onto a backing of burlap. He called his invention "linoleum"— from the Latin words *linum* ("flax") and *oleum* ("oil")—to be used as floor covering.

Perfecting the process, Walton combined "linoleum cement" (made from linseed oil and certain resins) with cork powder, wood flour, minerals, and color pigments to make "linoleum material," which he then applied by heat and pressure to a finely woven burlap base. He would then bake the linoleum in a huge oven for three to six weeks, curing it into hardened, finished linoleum.

Walton patented his process and opened the Linoleum Manufacturing Company in London in 1864 and the American Linoleum Manufacturing Company in New York City in 1872, but he failed to trademark the name linoleum. When Walton sued a competitor for using the name (but a different manufacturing process), the court ruled that linoleum had become a generic term.

NITROUS OXIDE

On December 10, 1844, Gardner Quincy Colton gave a public demonstration on the effects produced by inhaling nitrous oxide (better known as laughing gas) in Union Hall in Hartford, Connecticut. During his presentation, Colton offered to administer laughing gas to anyone who wished to inhale it and experience its intoxicating effects—for the audience's amusement.

Samuel A. Cooley, a druggist's assistant, was among those who volunteered. "While under its exhilarating influence he began to dance and jump about," recalled Colton in his book, *Boyhood and Manhood Recollections.* "He ran against some wooden settees on the stage, and bruised his shins badly."

As the effects of the gas subsided, Cooley returned to his seat next to his friend Horace Wells, a local dentist, who asked Cooley whether he had hurt himself. Cooley suddenly began to feel some pain and was astonished to find his legs all bloody.

Dr. Wells wondered if the laughing gas could be used to make a dental patient insensitive enough to extract a tooth painlessly. He asked Colton to bring a bag of nitrous oxide to his dental office the following day. Wells invited his colleague, Dr. John Riggs, to extract his decayed molar after he inhaled the nitrous oxide. Witnesses, including Colton and Riggs, testified that Riggs extracted the tooth while Wells was unconscious from inhaling the gas and that upon regaining consciousness, Wells insisted he had experienced no pain. "It is the greatest discovery ever made," Wells said. "I didn't feel it so much as the prick of a pin!" Wells had discovered the use of anesthesia in dentistry.

WISH-BONE SALAD DRESSING

In 1945, Phillip Sollomi, a soldier returning from World War II, opened a family-style chicken restaurant in Kansas City, Missouri, and named it "The Wish-Bone." Three years later, he asked his mother, an immigrant from Sicily, Italy, for the recipe for her spicy salad dressing. When customers at The Wish-Bone began asking for bottles of the salad dressing for use at home, Sollomi mixed the dressing in a fifty-gallon drum and bottled it  for sale in the restaurant. His mother happily applied labels reading "The Kansas City Wish-Bone Famous Italian-Style Dressing."

When salad dressing sales skyrocketed, Sollomi sold the restaurant and went into the salad dressing business, selling four varieties: Italian, Russian, French, and Cheese. In 1957, Lipton purchased the business, added new varieties (including Thousand Island), and marketed Wish-Bone Salad Dressings nationwide. In 1970, Wish-Bone became the best-selling Italian dressing in the United States, a position it holds to this day.

POTOSÍ

I n 1543, an Inca named Diego Huallpa, searching for an escaped llama at nightfall, stopped to build a fire on the slopes of the Andean mountain in Bolivia known in Quechua as *Potojsi* (meaning "thunder" or "explosion"). The next morning Huallpa discovered that rivulets of shiny silver liquid had percolated up from the ground beneath the fire during the night.

Huallpa immediately recognized the molten metal as silver, a commodity eagerly sought after by the Spanish conquistadors who had colonized his country. He tried to conceal his discovery from the Spaniards, hoping to mine the silver in secret, but one of his cohorts spread the news.

Upon learning of the enormous wealth buried in the mountain of Potojsi, the Spanish founded the city of Potosí in 1545 (giving it the illustrious name Villa Imperial de Carlos V) at the foot of the mountain they called Cerro Rico. The Spanish began large-scale mining operations, commandeering thousands of slaves to mine the silver so the bounty could be shipped to King Carlos V of Spain. Potosí was soon the largest city in the Americas with some 200,000 inhabitants.

No one knows whether Diego Huallpa ever found the missing llama.

DECLARATION OF INDEPENDENCE

(FIRST PRINTING)

n the summer of 1989, an anonymous Philadelphia financial analyst bought a torn painting of an old country scene for four dollars at a flea market in Adamstown, Pennsylvania, because he wanted the frame. When he got home, he removed the frame from the painting and found a first printing of the Declaration of Independence folded and hidden in the backing.

On July 4, 1776, John Dunlap of Philadelphia printed an estimated two hundred typeset copies of the Declaration of Independence, of which only twenty-four copies were known to have survived as of 1989. The Pennsylvania man had discovered number twenty-five.

Several months later, at the urging of a friend, the financial analyst called Sotheby's, the New York auction house, to have the document authenticated and appraised. Two years later, Sotheby's auctioned the copy for $2.42 million to Donald J. Scheer of Atlanta, Georgia, president of a fine arts investment firm. In 2000, Sotheby's auctioned the same document again for $8.14 million to an undisclosed buyer.

SACCHARIN

n June 1878, postdoctoral researcher Constantin Fahlberg, experimenting with coal tar derivatives in the Johns Hopkins University laboratory of chemistry professor Ira Remsen, spilled an experimental compound on his hands. "I was so interested in my laboratory that I forgot about my supper till quite late, and then rushed off for a meal without stopping to wash my hands," Fahlberg told *American Analyst* in 1886. "I sat down, broke a piece of bread, and put it to my lips. It tasted unspeakably sweet. I did not ask why it was so, probably because I thought it was some cake or sweetmeat. I rinsed my mouth with water, and dried my moustache with my napkin, when, to my surprise the napkin tasted sweeter than the bread. . . .

It flashed on me that I was the cause of the singular universal sweetness, and I accordingly tasted the end of my thumb, and found it surpassed any confectionery I had ever eaten."

Fahlberg immediately realized that he had happened upon some coal tar substance that was sweeter than sugar. Recognizing the commercial potential of the substance as a sweetener, he ran back to Remsen's laboratory, and "There, in my excitement, I tasted the contents of every beaker and evaporating dish on the table. Luckily for me, none contained any corrosive or poisonous liquid."

After locating the source (a beaker of benzoic sulfinide), Fahlberg detailed how he had synthesized the compound. In 1879, Fahlberg and Remsen published a coauthored article describing two methods of synthesizing saccharin. Without consulting Remsen, Fahlberg patented a new process in 1885, named the sweetener *saccharin* (Latin for "sugar"), and set up a factory in Germany to produce the noncaloric sweetener in both pill and powder form. In a letter to a friend, Remsen wrote, "Fahlberg is a scoundrel."

Today, Sweet'N Low, launched in 1957, is the Number One selling brand of saccharin in the United States.

DAGUERREOTYPE

One morning in 1837, French theater set designer Louis Daguerre, attempting to perfect the art of producing photographic images, entered his home laboratory, went to the chemical cabinet, and took out the silver-coated copper plate that he had exposed through a camera lens and left the night before. To Daguerre's surprise, the plate had developed a clear, sharp image.

Daguerre searched the cabinet to determine which chemical had developed the photographic plate, but the cabinet was filled with vials. That evening he removed one chemical from the cabinet and placed another exposed plate in the cabinet. In the morning, he found that that plate had developed, too. Daguerre eliminated one chemical each night—until one chemical remained. But when Daguerre tried that sole chemical on another exposed plate, it had no effect.

Baffled, Daguerre decided to place an exposed plate in the empty cabinet. In the morning, the plate was developed. Searching the cabinet thoroughly, he found a small puddle of mercury, spilled from a bottle, on one of the shelves. He tested it, confirming that the developing agent was indeed mercury vapor.

Daguerre named the developing process the daguerreotype—after himself. The daguerreotype became the first successful commercial photographic process, launching the photography industry.

VASELINE

n 1859, Robert Augustus Chesebrough, a 22-year-old Brooklyn chemist whose kerosene business faced impending closure, traveled to Titusville, Pennsylvania, to enter the competing petroleum business. Intrigued by the jelly residue that gunked up drilling rods, Chesebrough learned from workers that the jelly quickened healing when rubbed on a wound or burn. Chesebrough brought jars of the whipped gunk back to Brooklyn where he purified the petroleum lard into a clear, smooth gel that he called "petroleum jelly," which he began marketing in 1870 under the brand name Vaseline, a combination of the words *wasser* (Greek for "water") and *elaion* (Greek for "olive oil").

Within ten years, a jar of Vaseline could be found in almost every household in America. New mothers used the petroleum jelly on their infants to prevent diaper rash. Medical professionals recommended it to treat cuts and burns. Explorer Robert Peary carried a jar of Vaseline on his journey to the North Pole to protect his skin from chapping and his mechanical equipment from rusting. Cosmetic manufacturers buy Vaseline petroleum jelly in bulk as a base for beauty creams. And pharmaceutical companies use Vaseline petroleum jelly as a base to create their own brands of salves and creams.

TEMPLE OF MITHRAS

During the London Blitz in 1940, Nazi Germany bombed London, England, relentlessly for fifty-seven consecutive days, devastating the city. After the war, when large areas of London lay in ruins, archaeologist William F. Grimes, appointed director of the London Museum in 1945, saw the rubble-strewn city as an opportunity to search for any sign of the ancient Roman town of Londinium, founded in 43 C.E.

In 1954, Grimes and his team of archaeologists discovered on Walbrook Street the ruins of the Temple of Mithras, built by the Romans sometime between 240 and 250 C.E. to worship the Persian sun god Mithras. Grimes excavated the site, unearthing marble sculptures of Mithras, the Roman wine god Bacchus, and the Greco-Egyptian god Serapis. Today, the Museum of London displays the artifacts. To build a seven-story office building over the site, Legal & General paid to have the ruins moved to Queen Victoria Street. In 2012, to make way for its headquarters, Bloomberg L.P. paid to move the temple back to its original site.

SLOAN'S LINIMENT

n 1871, Earl Sloan, a 23-year-old native of the village of Zanesfield, Ohio, and the son of a self-taught veterinarian who sold homemade horse liniment, took his father's liniment recipe and moved to Missouri, where his brother traded horses. Earl began selling the horse tonic locally, and its popularity prompted the two brothers to travel to fairs and carnivals to sell it. When a customer

used the liniment on himself to relieve his aches and pains and claimed that it was "good for man or beast," the Sloan brothers adopted the slogan to promote their product.

Encouraged by their success, Earl traveled to Chicago and advertised

Sloan's Liniment in newspapers and on streetcars as a remedy for muscle aches, arthritis, and rheumatism, resulting in huge sales. A few years later, he relocated to Boston, added the title "Dr." to his name, and through clever marketing, turned his liniment into a household staple. By 1904, he was a millionaire.

INFANT JAUNDICE CURE

I n the summer of 1956, Sister J. Ward, a nurse working in Rochford General Hospital in Essex, England, noticed that newborn babies with jaundice, when wheeled outdoors in the warm sunshine, would lose their yellow tint and return to good health. The nurse reported her observation to the doctors.

A few weeks later, a nurse sent a blood specimen from a deeply jaundiced baby to the laboratory to test the level of bilirubin in the blood. (An abnormal concentration of bilirubin in the blood signals that the baby's developing liver cannot yet filter it out properly.) The blood sample sat on the windowsill in the sunlight for several hours. When biochemist P. W. Perryman returned from lunch, he performed the test and reported the bilirubin level, which was significantly low for such a jaundiced baby. Shortly afterward, Perryman retested the sample, still lying in full sunlight on the windowsill and reported an even lower reading than before.

Subsequent research on the effects of sunlight on bilirubin revealed that visible blue light bathing the naked skin of the babies converted the bilirubin into a form babies could excrete. Irradiating infants with blue florescent light quickly became standard practice to prevent or cure infant jaundice.

LINDOW MAN

On August 6, 1984, commercial peat-cutter Andy Mould was cutting peat from Lindow Moss bog near the airport in Manchester, England, for use in gardens. When he fed a load of peat onto the conveyer belt of a milling machine, something fell off the conveyer belt, landing at Mould's feet. He picked up what he thought was a branch of hogwort and noticed toenails. Together with his colleagues, he brought the well-preserved leg and foot, which he said felt like "a piece of leather" to the local police station.

The police immediately closed the site to investigate a possible murder. Anatomists, archaeologists, anthropologists, and botanists descended on the site, identified the leg and foot as prehistoric remains, and eventually recovered the rest of the body—one of the most perfectly preserved ancient human beings ever found.

The acidic, oxygen-free conditions in the peat bog had preserved the man's skin, hair, and many of his internal organs.

Transported to the British Museum and thoroughly examined by a team of scientists, Lindow Man has yielded more information than any other prehistoric person found in Britain. Radiocarbon dating showed that this Celtic man died between 2 B.C.E. and 119 C.E. when he was roughly twenty-five years old. His manicured fingernails suggested that he performed very little manual labor, and his beard and moustache appeared to have been trimmed with a pair of shears.

Forensic examination suggested that Lindow Man had been the victim of a ritual killing, possibly a human sacrifice carried out by Druids. He died after being bludgeoned on the head, suffering a broken rib, and being strangled with a thin cord.

Lindow Man, freeze-dried for preservation and stored in a climate-controlled cabinet, can be viewed in the British Museum in London.

SLINKY

n 1943, Richard James, a 29-year-old marine engineer working in Philadelphia's Cramp Shipyard, tried to figure out how to use springs to mount delicate meters on World War II battleships. One day a torsion spring accidentally fell off his desk and tumbled end over end across the floor. James realized he could create a new toy by devising a steel formula that would give the spring the proper tension to "walk."

After James found a steel wire that would coil, uncoil, and recoil, his wife, Betty, a graduate of Penn State University, thumbed through the dictionary to find an appropriate name for the toy.

She chose Slinky because the word meant "stealthy, sleek, and sinuous."

In 1945, the Jameses borrowed $500 to pay a machine shop to make a small quantity of Slinkys. During the Christmas shopping season, they convinced a buyer from Gimbels Department Store in downtown Philadelphia to provide counter space for four hundred Slinkys and let them demonstrate the new toy to customers. Richard James went alone, carrying a small demonstration staircase. Much to his astonishment, he sold all four hundred Slinkys in ninety minutes.

The Slinky became the hit of the 1946 American Toy Fair, and Slinky sales soared. The Jameses opened a factory in Philadelphia, and Richard invented machines that could coil eighty feet of steel wire into a Slinky in less than eleven seconds.

In 1960, Richard James abandoned his business and family to join a religious cult in Bolivia, leaving his wife, Betty, behind with six kids. Betty James relocated the Slinky factory to her hometown of Hollidaysburg, Pennsylvania, and began marketing the toy in television commercials with a catchy jingle that turned the Slinky into one of the most popular toys in the world.

CAESAR SALAD

Over the Fourth of July weekend in 1924, restaurateur Caesar Cardini ran low on food at his restaurant in Tijuana, Mexico. Cardini quickly tossed together leftover ingredients from his kitchen—romaine lettuce, garlic, croutons, Parmesan cheese, boiled eggs, olive oil, and Worcestershire sauce—to improvise a salad for his guests on a service cart at tableside. He made the salad dressing first, then coated the leaves of romaine lettuce and placed them stem-side out in a circle on a dinner plate, so that the guest could pick up each leaf with his fingers.

In 1926, Cardini's brother Alex, an ace pilot in the Italian air force during World War I, joined his brother at the Tijuana restaurant and added other ingredients to Caesar's Salad, including anchovies.

Mrs. Wallis Warfield Simpson, mistress and ultimately wife of Prince Edward VIII of Wales (later king of England), visited Hotel Caesar's Place, became enraptured with Caesar Salad, and subsequently insisted that the chefs at many of the great European restaurants make it for her. In 1948, Caesar Cardini received a patent on the dressing, which is still bottled and sold as "Cardini's Original Caesar Dressing," distributed by Caesar Cardini Foods of Culver City, California.

REGENERATIVE CIRCUIT

I n the summer of 1912, Edwin Howard Armstrong, a 22-year-old Columbia University electrical engineering student living at home with his family in Yonkers, New York, rewired his crystal radio receiver, tuned in on some signals, and heard them without putting on his earphones. Armstrong diligently examined his circuit and discovered that he had accidentally rearranged the plate coil and grid coil of the tube, placing them closer together. He theorized that the current from the plate coil was feeding back into the grid coil, amplifying the signals.

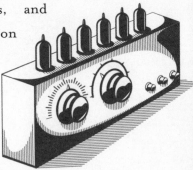

After testing his theory for two months and receiving radio signals from Ireland and Hawaii with astounding clarity, Armstrong asked his father for money to register a patent. His father refused, convinced that his son needed to pay more attention to his studies and stop fiddling with the radio. Undaunted, Armstrong drew up a detailed wiring diagram and had it notarized, establishing his claim to the discovery of the regenerative circuit, which became and remained a standard feature of radio receivers. He graduated from Columbia University in 1913.

SAFETY GLASS

n 1903, French chemist Édouard Bénédictus climbed a ladder to retrieve chemicals from a shelf and accidentally dropped a glass flask onto the hard floor. The flask shattered, but the shards of glass did not fly apart. Instead, the shattered glass retained the original shape of the flask.

Baffled, Bénédictus examined the shattered flask and discovered a thin film coating the inside. The broken shards of glass remained adhered to the film. Bénédictus learned that the flask had previously contained a solution of collodion, which had evaporated, leaving behind the clear film. He labeled the flask and stored it on a shelf.

Shortly afterward, Bénédictus read several newspaper stories about people who had been badly cut by flying glass from windshields in automobile accidents in Paris. He suddenly realized that the non-shattering flask might help prevent such accidents. He returned to the laboratory and used a letterpress to bond a sheet of collodion between two sheets of glass, producing the first sheet of safety glass.

Automobile manufacturers initially refused to use costly safety glass for windshields, preferring instead to curtail the price of cars. During World War I, gas mask manufacturers used safety glass as the lenses to better protect soldiers. When automobile makers beheld the virtues of safety glass under battle conditions, they quickly embraced the use of safety glass for car windshields.

CARTESIAN PLANE

hile lying in bed one morning in the 1600s, French philosopher and mathematician René Descartes noticed a fly walking across the ceiling. He watched the fly for a long time and wondered how he could describe the fly's path along the ceiling without tracing its path. Descartes realized that he could precisely describe the position of the fly anywhere in the room by noting its perpendicular distances from two adjacent walls and from the ceiling.

When he got out of bed, Descartes wrote down his observation and attempted to describe the coordinates of various points in the same way he had described the co-

ordinates of the fly. In doing so, he invented coordinate geometry, tying together the two great branches of mathematics: algebra and geometry. The coordinate plane, considered one of the most revolutionary and profound ideas in history, is also called the Cartesian plane in Descartes' honor.

I n 1945, with just $500, ex-magician Benjamin Hirsch set up shop in a small Chicago storefront at 2207 Chicago Avenue, where he developed Plastone Liquid Car Polish by mixing batches of his solution in a bathtub. His wife and partner, Marie, would bottle the polish, and Ben would sell it. To sell Plastone Liquid Car

Polish, Hirsch would often wax parked cars while waiting for the owner to return.

In the early 1950s, while driving home from a sales call in Beloit, Wisconsin, Hirsch stopped to rest at a place named Turtle Creek, rested by a stream, and was suddenly struck by his reflection in the water. Realizing that his car polish provided a wax coating as tough as a turtle shell and as reflective as Turtle Creek, he renamed his product Turtle Wax.

Turtle Wax, Inc., is frequently offered supplies of turtles. Former company president, Carl Schmid, would politely refuse these offers, pointing out that the turtles in Turtle Wax are like the horses in horseradish.

ROSETTA STONE

n July 1799, French soldiers in Napoleon's army were ordered to demolish a wall at Fort St. Julien near the town of Rashíd (Rosetta), Egypt, roughly forty miles east of Alexandria, to clear the way to lay a foundation for an extension of the fort. Embedded in the wall, the soldiers discovered a stone inscribed in three different scripts: hieroglyphic, demotic (native Egyptian script), and Greek.

Lieutenant Pierre François Xavier Bouchard and his fellow officers on the demolition team immediately realized that the three inscriptions on this stone contained the same text translated into three different scripts, and the Greek might be used to decipher both the hieroglyphs and demotic writings. (Egyptians ceased using hieroglyphs in 394 C.E. and stopped using demotic Egyptian in 452 C.E. Knowledge of how to read and write both hieroglyphs and demotic Egyptian vanished soon afterward.)

The French moved the stone to Cairo in August, and scholars used the Greek inscription to decode the dead languages.

The Rosetta Stone, inscribed in 196 B.C.E., on the first anniversary of the coronation of Ptolemy V, a Greek who became pharaoh of Egypt at age six, declares Ptolemy's new status as a living god. English physicist Thomas Young showed that some of the hieroglyphs on the Rosetta Stone depict the sounds of the name Ptolemy. French scholar Jean-François Champollion then realized that hieroglyphs recorded the sound of the ancient Egyptian language.

Upon Napoleon's defeat, the Treaty of Alexandria gave the Rosetta Stone and other antiquities seized by the French to the British. The Rosetta Stone is on exhibit in the British Museum in London.

FRITOS CORN CHIPS

n 1932, Charles Elmer Doolin, a confectioner who made pies and cakes in his family's store and cafe in San Antonio, Texas, stopped for lunch at a small café. He bought a plain package of fried corn chips made from corn dough, used for centuries to make tortillas in Mexico. Six years later, Doolin tracked down the maker of the corn chips and bought the recipe and the manufacturing equipment—a converted hand-operated potato slicer—using one hundred dollars that he borrowed from his mother Daisy, who, according to legend, pawned her wedding ring to get it. He imagined that the *fritos* ("little fried things") would be served as a side dish with soup and salad—never

anticipating that they would become a popular stand-alone snack food that would be available in a family-size bag.

Doolin produced Fritos Corn Chips in his mother's kitchen, making ten pounds of chips per hour, and sold the chips out of the back of his Model T Ford, earning a profit as high as two dollars a day.

In 1945, the Frito Company, distributing Fritos Corn Chips across the Southwest, granted H. W. Lay & Company, the maker of Lay's Potato Chips, the right to manufacture and distribute Fritos Corn Chips in the Southeast. In 1961, the two companies merged to form Frito-Lay, Inc.

THE BEATLES

n April 1960 in Liverpool, England, former art students John Lennon and Stuart Sutcliffe named their band "The Beatles"—inspired by the way the name of Buddy Holly's band, The Crickets, seemed to play off cricket the game and cricket the insect. "We were thrilled with that," recalled Paul McCartney in *The Beatles Anthology*. "We thought it was true literature."

"Stu was really into Marlon Brando," remembered George Harrison, "and in the movie *The Wild One*, there is a scene where Lee Marvin says: 'Johnny, we've been looking for you, the Beetles have missed you, all the Beetles have missed you.'

Maybe John and Stu were both thinking about it at the time."

"I was looking for a name like The Crickets that meant two things," recalled Lennon in a 1964 interview, "and from crickets I got to beetles. And I changed the BEA, because 'beetles' didn't mean two things on its own. When you said it, people thought of crawly things; and when you read it, it was beat music."

After achieving worldwide fame, the Beatles met The Crickets who had no idea cricket was a game in England or that their name had a second meaning.

POP-UP TOASTER

During World War I, factory mechanic Charles Strite grew tired of eating the burnt toast served in the company cafeteria in Stillwater, Minnesota. Exasperated, he rigged a variable timer to a spring release and heating coils to create the world's first pop-up toaster—making Strite the toast of the town. The heating elements toasted both sides of the bread simultaneously. The timer turned off the electricity and triggered a spring to eject the finished toast from the device.

After Strite received a patent for his invention in 1919, the Childs restaurant chain placed an order for the first batch of one hundred pop-up toasters (assembled by hand). Unfortunately, Childs had to return every toaster to be mechanically adjusted.

In 1926, Strite introduced the Toastmaster, the first pop-up toaster for the home—complete with a dial to adjust to the desired degree of darkness. Unfortunately, the Toastmaster grew hotter after making each slice of toast. The first slice popped up underdone, and the sixth slice popped up burnt. Strite eventually perfected his toaster, selling more than one million by 1930.

SMALLPOX VACCINATION

I n 1768, a former milkmaid told nineteen-year-old Edward Jenner, an apprentice working under surgeon Daniel Ludlow in Chipping Sodbury, England, that she could never get smallpox because she had contracted and survived cowpox, a mild viral infection of cows.

Four years later, after completing his medical training at St. George's Hospital in London, Jenner returned to his hometown of Berkeley in Gloucestershire and opened a medical practice. Realizing the futility of trying to treat smallpox and recalling the comment that milkmaid had made years earlier, he conducted an investigation and discovered that milkmaids

rarely contracted smallpox—even when they came into frequent contact with someone suffering from the disease. He then wondered if inoculating patients with cowpox might give them immunity from smallpox.

In May 1796, when dairymaid Sarah Nelmes consulted Jenner about a rash on her hand, he diagnosed the condition as cowpox and took the opportunity to test his theory. He drew some matter from one of the pockmarks on Nelmes's hand, and on May 14, he made a few scratches on the arm of eight-year-old James Phipps, the son of his gardener, and rubbed the matter into them. A few days later, James came down with a mild bout of cowpox, returning to health within a week. On July 1, to test whether the cowpox would now protect James from smallpox, Jenner inoculated James with smallpox matter. The boy did not develop smallpox.

Jenner conducted his experiment successfully on others, and in 1798, he announced that an inoculation of cowpox does indeed provide immunity against smallpox. In 1980, the World Health Organization announced that the smallpox vaccine had eradicated smallpox from the earth.

BRAZIL

On March 9, 1500, King Manuel I of Portugal sent navigator Pedro Alvares Cabral on the second major expedition to India with 13 ships and 1,200 men. Cabral sailed southwest past the African coast and then

turned west into the Atlantic Ocean to take advantage of the prevailing winds and currents. The explorer swung too far west, crossing the Atlantic Ocean at its narrowest point and accidentally discovering Brazil.

Cabral sighted Monte Pascoal, a rounded mountain on the Brazilian coast, sailed north for three days, and anchored near what is now Porto Seguro. On April 21, Cabral sent a search party ashore, and the next day, he named the newly discovered "island" Ilha de Vera Cruz and claimed it for Portugal. Eight days later, Cabral began the trip back across the Atlantic to round the Cape of Good Hope and continue on toward Calicut on the west coast of India.

In 1501, Portuguese explorer Gonzalo Coelho explored the Brazilian coast with Amerigo Vespucci as his chronicler. The Portuguese did not settle Brazil for another twenty-five years because the land, while fertile and sparsely populated by primitive Tupinambá Indians, lacked rich trade cities, precious metals, and a significant source of slave labor. The demand for Brazil wood, a source of red dye desired by Europeans, ultimately prompted Portugal to colonize the land and rename it Brazil.

INKJET PRINTER

I n August 1977, Ichiro Endo, an engineer at the Canon company in Japan, accidentally dropped a soldering iron onto an ink syringe sitting on the workbench. A few moments later, he noticed ink jetting from the tip of the syringe. Realizing that the heat had boiled the ink, causing bubbles to shoot it out through the nozzle, Endo attempted to recreate the incident and used a special high-speed camera to record the details of the phenomenon.

Canon had assigned Endo's team, consisting of some

forty researchers, the task of seeking alternatives to conventional xerographic printing, and the group had been experimenting with existing inkjet technologies. Within three days of Endo's fortuitous accident with the soldering iron, his team used his discovery to build a working thermal bubble-jet device.

To print a document, an inkjet printer sends a pulse of electrical current to heat a series of tiny chambers, causing a small explosion of steam in each chamber to form a bubble, propelling a droplet of ink onto the paper. The suction created by the contraction of the steam bubble pulls more ink into the cartridge from an attached ink reservoir.

POST-IT NOTES

n 1974, Art Fry, a researcher in product development at 3M, sang each Sunday with his choir at North Presbyterian Church in North St. Paul, Minnesota. He marked the pages of his hymnal with scraps of paper, but the scraps kept falling out, forcing him to constantly scramble to find his place.

"I don't know if it was a dull sermon or divine inspiration," Fry recalled in *Our Story So Far*, "but my mind began to wander and suddenly I thought of an adhesive that had been discovered years earlier by another 3M scientist, Dr. Spencer Silver." While researching ways to develop stronger, high-tack adhesives, Silver had accidentally discovered an

adhesive that wasn't very sticky. At the time, no one had any idea what to do with it.

Fry went to work on Monday morning and applied some of Silver's "not-so-sticky" glue to the edge of a piece of paper. One end stuck to the page of his book, the other end stuck out like a bookmark. Fry could also easily reposition the bookmark without damaging the pages. When Fry wrote a note on one of his new bookmarks and attached it to a report he was forwarding to his supervisor, he realized that his sticky bookmark was actually a new way to pass notes. But 3M company management had no interest in producing a note pad that would sell for a premium price when people could just as easily use ordinary scratch paper.

Fry passed out samples of the sticky little pieces of paper to the secretaries at 3M, figuring they were the people in the company most likely to find uses for them. The secretaries were quickly hooked on Fry's "press and peel notes" and soon demanded more. Fry couldn't keep up with the increasing demand, and finally, at the urging of their own secretaries, the top brass gave Fry the green light to produce Post-it Notes.

SUPER SOAKER

n 1982, while trying to devise a heat pump that utilized water instead of Freon, NASA nuclear engineer Lonnie G. Johnson accidentally used pressurized air to send a stream of water across his bathroom and into the tub.

"I thought, 'This would make a great water gun,'" he told the Associated Press in 1999. Johnson decided to build a high-tech squirt gun engineered with an air pump that would enable a child to pump up the squirt gun with compressed air.

Johnson created the prototype in his basement workshop near Edwards Air Force Base in California, using PVC pipe, Plexiglas, and an empty Coke bottle. After letting his six-year-old daughter test his "Power

Drencher" on neighbors, Johnson arranged a meeting at the Larami Corporation, a toy company, where he opened a battered pink Samsonite suitcase, took out his Power Drencher, and fired a powerful stream of water across the boardroom, blasting coffee cups off the table.

Larami agreed to distribute the renamed Super Soaker to stores. Just before Christmas in 1990 on *The Tonight Show*, Johnny Carson used one to blast his audience and sidekick Ed McMahon. The publicity helped transform the Super Soaker into the best-selling water gun in American history and Lonnie Johnson into a multimillionaire.

CLASSICAL CONDITIONING

n 1901 at the Institute of Experimental Medicine in St. Petersburg, Russia, physiologist Ivan Pavlov was studying the digestive system in dogs to qualify the relationship between the amount of food eaten and the secretions of digestive juices. He noticed that the animals would salivate to the sights and sounds associated with the delivery of food, such as his laboratory assistant entering the room or the clanging of metal food carts being wheeled into the laboratory—even if no food was being delivered.

Pavlov theorized that the stimuli associated with feeding triggered the salivation reflex. He called this response a "conditioned reflex," meaning it was learned. He trained a dog to salivate at the sound of a bell by presenting the sound (the stimulus) just moments before food was brought into the room. Eventually the dog began to salivate—producing the conditioned response—at the sound of the bell alone.

Pavlov dedicated the rest of his life to studying this form of learning, which we now call classical conditioning. Classical conditioning techniques are sometimes used to treat phobias and anxiety problems.

NAZCA LINES

In 1926, Peruvian archaeologist Toribio Mejîa Xesspe and American archaeologist Alfred Kroeber, climbed a hill near the Peruvian town of Nazca to search the Cantalloc burial site. Stopping to catch their breath and admire the view, they noticed that the landscape was

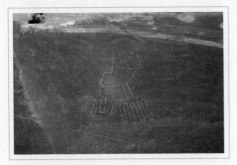

covered with strange markings—vast lines that could only be seen in their entirety from nearby foothills or from high in the sky. Kroeber described

these features in a report and ascribed the lines to religious processions or games.

More than a decade later, pilots of the Peruvian air force flew over the region and took photographs, confirming the existence of the enormous network of lines and images spanning eighty-five square miles and depicting hundreds of shapes, including jaguars, monkeys, and spiders. The lines, created sometime between 300 B.C.E. and 540 C.E., were made by removing the thin, topmost layer of dark pebbles to reveal the yellowish-white soil beneath. The dry, windless desert preserved the drawings for millennia.

The mystery of the Nazca lines lies in the enormous scale and complexity of the designs. German mathematician and archaeologist Maria Reiche, who spent her lifetime examining the lines, proposed that the lines were some type of celestial calendar, marking the appearance of certain constellations. Reich theorized that the Nazca people created their complex system of designs by reproducing small drawings on a grand scale using ropes and stone markers.

GRANOLA AND CORN FLAKES

n 1898, Dr. John Harvey Kellogg directed the Adventist Battle Creek Sanitarium in Battle Creek, Michigan. A Seventh-day Adventist, Kellogg invented various health foods based on Adventist beliefs in health care, with help from his brother, William Keith Kellogg. While trying to invent a more digestible form of bread, he accidentally left some boiled wheat paste to sit out overnight. In the morning, the Kellogg brothers ran the dried wheat dough through rollers and baked it, accidentally creating crispy granola flakes, which they

called Granose and served as a cereal to patients at the sanitarium. William continued experimenting, ultimately flaking corn.

In 1905, after making a fortune selling Granose and Sanitas Toasted Corn Flakes (produced in a barn on the sanitarium grounds), the Kellogg brothers had a disagreement over who had authorized William Kellogg to spend $50,000 to build a new factory. Left holding the bag for the factory, William added cane sugar to the recipe for corn flakes cereal, started the Battle Creek Toasted Corn Flake Company, and advertised the cereal heavily—turning Kellogg's Corn Flakes into a $5.7 million company by the 1930s.

RADIOACTIVITY

n 1896, following a discussion with French physicist Henri Poincaré regarding the X-rays recently discovered by Wilhelm Conrad Röntgen, French physicist Antoine Henri Becquerel, a professor at the École Polytechnique in Paris, decided to investigate whether substances made phosphorescent by sunlight might then emit a penetrating radiation similar to X-rays. Having inherited from his physicist father a supply of uranium salts, which phosphoresce when exposed to light, Becquerel wrapped a photographic plate in opaque black paper (to shield the plate from any light), set the wrapped plate in the sunlight, and placed a uranium crystal on top of it. When he developed

the photographic plate, an image of the uranium crystal appeared.

Convinced that he had proven that sunlight activated the phosphorescence of the uranium crystal (and unable to continue his experiments for several days due to overcast skies in Paris), Becquerel put the uranium crystal in a drawer on top of a photographic plate wrapped in opaque paper. Several days later, he developed the photographic plate, expecting to find a faint image of the crystal due to the waning phosphorescence of the uranium crystal. Instead, he found an image of the crystal as strong as the one he created by sitting the crystal and the wrapped plate in the sunlight. Becquerel concluded that his theory had been wrong. The uranium crystal, without the aid of sunlight, had exposed the photograph plate. He had accidentally discovered radioactivity.

CELLULOID

In 1863, a major shortage of ivory prompted the firm of Phelan & Collender, a major manufacturer of billiard balls, to offer a $10,000 prize for the patent rights to anyone who developed an ivory substitute that could be used to make billiard balls. Hoping to win the prize, John Wesley Hyatt, a printer in Albany, New York, and his brother Isaiah began experimenting with a mixture of

sawdust and paper bonded together with glue.

When John Hyatt accidentally cut his finger while working on the project, he went to the cupboard to get a bottle of collodion (a dilute form of cellulose nitrate commonly used at the time to protect minor wounds with a hard, thin film). Hyatt discovered that the bottle had tipped over, spilled, and dried in the cupboard, leaving a solidified puddle of cellulose nitrate on the shelf. He realized that the collodion might work better than glue to create his sawdust and paper billiard ball.

The Hyatt brothers soon discovered that collodion evaporated slowly, shrinking and cracking as it dried. In 1869, John Hyatt decided to use solid camphor as a solvent to hasten evaporation of wet cellulose nitrate (pulped cotton nitrated in acid). He mixed ground camphor with cellulose nitrate, heated the mixture, and then compacted it into a mold. When it cooled, Hyatt had produced a hard, durable, shiny substance that his brother Isaiah named celluloid (a combination of the words *cellulose* and *collodion*).

The Hyatts patented and trademarked their plastic, and although no one ever received the $10,000 prize, the Hyatts profited from the use of celluloid to manufacture dental plates, billiard balls, dominoes, knife and brush handles, combs, piano keys, dice, fountain pens, and celluloid collars for men's shirts.

IODINE

n 1811, French chemist Bernard Courtois ran a factory near Paris that manufactured saltpeter (potassium nitrate). Seeking a cheaper source of potassium than wood ash, Courtois located potassium in the seaweed that washed up on the Atlantic coast of France. After workers burned the seaweed in tanks to extract potassium from the ash, they occasionally had to clean the tanks with acid to remove accumulated sludge.

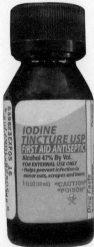

One day, the workers used a stronger acid to clean the tanks, causing violet fumes to rise from the tanks. Dark, metallic-looking crystals appeared wherever the violet vapor came into contact with cold surfaces. Awed by this strange occurrence, Courtois collected some crystals and gave them to

Charles Desormes and Nicolas Clément—two chemist friends at the École Polytechnique in Paris.

After Desormes and Clément described the crystalline substance in a paper published in December 1813, eminent French chemist Joseph Louis Gay-Lussac obtained a sample of the crystals from Courtois. Soon afterward, Gay-Lussac announced the discovery of a new element, suggesting the name *iode* (from the Greek word for "violet"). British chemist Sir Humphrey Davy confirmed Gay-Lussac's findings and suggested the name "iodine"—to make the name conform to the recently named element chlorine.

Seaweed contains the salts sodium chloride, sodium iodide, and potassium iodide. Biochemical processes in seaweed concentrate the iodide salts, and burning the seaweed concentrates them further. The strong acid Courtois used to clean the tanks changed the concentrated iodide salts to elemental iodine, and the heat from the chemical reaction vaporized the iodine. When the iodine vapor touched cool surfaces, it condensed to a crystalline form.

LUCY

Late one afternoon in November 1973 in Hadar, Ethiopia, American paleoanthropologist Donald Johanson was searching the desert for elephant teeth. "I idly kicked at what looked like a hippo rib sticking up in the sand," he recalled in his book, *Lucy: The Beginnings of Humankind*. Upon closer inspection, Johanson realized that the bone was actually the upper end of a shinbone from a small primate. "A monkey, I thought, and decided to collect it." A few yards away, he noticed the lower end of a thighbone, which fit together with the first bone to form a knee joint at an angle, characteristic of human

knees—meaning this hominid walked upright. Testing revealed that the knee joint was more than three million years old.

The following year, Johanson returned to Hadar, and in November 1974, while crossing ground they had searched many times before, Johanson and graduate student Tom Gray noticed parts of a leg bone, a piece of jaw, and a skull fragment.

A meticulous search followed, and after several weeks of excavation, Johanson and his colleagues unearthed several hundred pieces of bone, all of which belonged to a single adult female who stood a mere three feet eight inches tall and represented the most complete and oldest prehistoric human ancestor known at the time. Johanson named the skeleton Lucy after the Beatles song "Lucy in the Sky With Diamonds," which was played in the camp when the scientists celebrated their discovery. Radiometric dating placed Lucy's age at approximately 3.2 million years. The nature of Lucy's knees and pelvic bones provide compelling evidence that our human ancestors stood upright long before our brains enlarged—making Lucy a landmark fossil find.

PHONOGRAPH

n 1877, thirty-year-old Thomas Alva Edison attempted to develop an automatic telegraph repeater that would record incoming messages—by embossing strips of paper with the appropriate dots and dashes—and mechanically send them out again to another telegraph station. Working in his laboratory in Menlo Park, New Jersey, he noticed that the vibration of the telegraph instrument lever produced an audible note whenever the embossed strip of paper was gently pulled beneath it. He immediately reasoned that, if the paper strip could be imprinted with elevations and depressions representative of sound waves, it might be used to actuate a diaphragm to mechanically reproduce the corresponding sound.

Edison ceased his work on the telegraph repeater and focused all his attention on developing the phonograph. He designed a machine with a diaphragm mouthpiece connected to an embossing point and a hand-cranked cylinder wrapped in a sheet of tinfoil. The first words he recorded were "Mary had a little lamb." Ten years later, Edison substituted a permanent cylindrical wax record for the tinfoil and added a battery-powered electrical motor.

Edison's first phonograph is on display in the Victoria and Albert Museum in London, England.

TOMB OF MARQUIS YI OF ZENG

n 1977, the Chinese army, leveling a hill to build a factory in Suizhou, accidentally discovered a tomb with four chambers built of large wooden timbers and connected by small doors. Marquis Yi of Zeng, a fifth-century B.C.E. Chinese ruler, was buried in the tomb along with a bianzhong (a set of sixty-four bronze bells mounted on a lacquered wood frame), a sixty-fifth bell sent as a gift by the king of Chu, a thirty-two-chime lithophone, forty stringed instruments, and twenty-one young women to play them in the afterlife.

Prior to the discovery of the well-preserved

tomb, all records of Marquis Yi of Zeng, a vassal of the Chu kingdom, had been lost to history. The 15,000 relics in the tomb—including gold dishes and jade jewelry—provided archaeologists with invaluable information on ancient China. The main chamber contained the musical instruments (including bamboo flutes, panpipes, mouth organs, and drums), a bedchamber housed the coffin, and the remaining two rooms held the female attendants and weaponry.

The bianzhong, the finest set of ancient chime bells ever discovered, produces a range of more than five octaves of twelve semitones each and has been compared to a modern-day piano. Archaeologists note that the precision with which the bells were cast illustrates the remarkable advances that the artisans had achieved.

The treasures from the tomb can been seen at the Hubei Provincial Museum in Wuhan, China.

CHOCOLATE CHIP COOKIES

n 1930, Ruth Graves Wakefield and her husband Kenneth purchased a Cape Cod-style cottage on the outskirts of Whitman, Massachusetts, halfway between Boston and New Bedford. Built in 1709, the house had served as a rest stop for road-weary travelers, who stopped there to pay tolls, change horses, and enjoy home-cooked

 meals. The Wakefields turned the house into a lodge and named it the Toll House Inn. Having worked as a dietitian and food lecturer,

Ruth cooked homemade meals and baked desserts for guests, attracting people from across New England.

Sometime in 1937, while preparing the batter for

Butter Drop Dough cookies, Ruth ran out of baker's chocolate. She found a semisweet chocolate bar (given to her by Andrew Nestlé, a friend who owned a chocolate factory), cut it into tiny bits, and added them to the dough, expecting the chocolate pieces to melt as the cookies baked in the oven. To Ruth's surprise, the chocolate did not melt, retaining its shape and softening to a creamy texture. Guests loved the cookies, and so Ruth continued baking what she called the "Toll House Crunch Cookie."

After a Boston newspaper published Ruth's recipe and Betty Crocker featured it on her national radio program in 1939, sales of Nestlé's Semi-Sweet Chocolate Bar soared. Ultimately, Nestlé bought the rights to print Ruth's recipe for the "Toll House Cookie" on the package of his Toll House Chocolate Morsels. In exchange, Ruth also received all the chocolate she could use for the rest of her life.

The chocolate chip cookie became the most popular cookie in America, and although the Toll House burned down in 1984, Nestlé still prints the cookie recipe on every package of Toll House Chocolate Morsels.

Q-TIPS

n 1922, Leo Gerstenzang, a Jewish immigrant from Warsaw, Poland, who had served in the U.S. Army during World War I and worked with the fledgling Red Cross organization, founded the Leo Gerstenzang Infant Novelty Co. with his wife, selling accessories used for baby care. After the birth of the couple's daughter in 1926, Gerstenzang noticed that his wife would 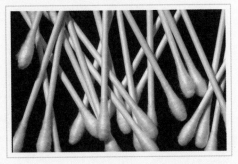 wrap a wad of cotton around a toothpick for use during their baby's bath. Inspired by this observation, he decided to manufacture a ready-to-use cotton swab.

After several years, Gerstenzang developed a machine that would wrap cotton uniformly around each blunt end of a small stick of carefully selected and cured non-splintering birch wood, package the swabs in a sliding tray type box, sterilize the box, and seal it with an outer wrapping of glassine (later changed to cellophane). The phrase "untouched by human hands" became widely known in the production of cotton swabs. Gerstenzang originally called the product Baby Gays, but soon he changed the name to Q-tips. The *Q* stands for "quality," and the word *tips* describes the cotton swab on the end of the stick.

QUININE

egend holds that a lone native South American, lost in a high jungle in the Andes, suffered a burning fever. He located a stagnant pool of water and drank the cool water, which tasted bitter. He realized that the water had been tainted by the bark of nearby quina-quina trees, which grow on the slopes of the Andes between Columbia and Bolivia at elevations above 5,000 feet.

Although native South Americans believed that the bark of the quina-quina tree was poisonous, the fevered man continued drinking the tainted water, indifferent to its potential deadliness. Miraculously, the man's fever subsided. Upon returning to

Cinchona Calisaya Weed.

his native village, he relayed how drinking from the tainted pool had cured his burning fever. From then on, natives used extracts from the bark of the quina-quina tree to treat intense fever. Unbeknownst to the natives, the fever was caused by malaria, and the bark of the quina-quina tree contained the chemical quinine.

A European legend tells that the Countess del Chinchón, the wife of the Peruvian envoy, was cured of malaria by taking an extract of the bark of the quina-quina tree. The countess purportedly brought samples of the bark back to Spain in 1640, introducing the use of quinine to Europe. In truth, the countess never had malaria and did not bring the bark to Spain. She died suddenly in Cartagena, Columbia, on January 14, 1641, before reaching Spain. Still, a century later in 1742, Swedish botanist Carl Linnaeus named the tree "Cinchona" in her honor.

In 1820, French chemists Pierre Joseph Pelletier and Joseph Bienaimé Caventou isolated the active antimalarial ingredient quinine from cinchona bark.

POPSICLE

On a cold winter night in 1905, eleven-year-old Frank Epperson accidentally left a glass of lemonade with a spoon in it outside on the porch. In the morning, he pulled on the spoon and out came the world's first "Epsicle." The enterprising young man began selling his ice pop to his school friends. Eighteen years later in 1923, Epperson, who ran a lemonade stand at an amusement park in

Alameda, California, applied for a patent for "frozen ice on a stick," which his children renamed Popsicle. By 1928, Epperson had earned royalties on more than sixty million Popsicles.

During the Depression, Epperson created the twin Popsicle so two children could

split it for a nickel. Epperson also invented the Fudgsicle, Creamsicle, and Dreamsicle. In the 1950s, when Popsicles boxed in a multipack were introduced to grocery stores, sales skyrocketed into the billions. As of 2013, there were more than thirty variations on the original Popsicle. The most popular Popsicle flavors are orange, cherry, and grape.

BLACK HILLS MAMMOTHS

n 1974, George Hanson operated an earthmover to excavate the land for a housing development on the outskirts of Hot Springs, a city near the Black Hills of southwestern South Dakota. Twenty feet beneath the surface, he unearthed a stockpile of large bones.

Hanson invited his son, Dan, who was taking a college geology class, to visit the sight. Dan stubbed his toe on what he recognized to be an exposed mammoth tooth. Dan reported the discovery to his former professor, Larry Agenbroad, who was teaching at

Chadron State College in Chadron, Nebraska. Agenbroad identified the bones as belonging to Columbian mammoths that had been trapped in a sinkhole 26,000 years earlier.

The landowner, Phil Anderson, stopped all construction on the site and gave Agenbroad and a group of volunteers permission to excavate further. The discovery of a mammoth skull with its tusks intact helped persuade Anderson to set the site aside for science, and Agenbroad helped the citizens of Hot Springs set up a nonprofit corporation and raise more than $1 million to buy the land and build a shelter over the archaeological site. To date, the Mammoth Site of Hot Springs has yielded sixty-one mammoth skeletons, making it the most impressive mammoth site in the Americas.

SUPER GLUE

n 1945, Dr. Harry Coover, working for Eastman Kodak's chemical division in Rochester, New York, worked with a team of researchers to find a way to make optically clear plastic for gun sights during World War II. Experimenting with chemicals known as cyanoacrylates, the team discovered that a minute amount of moisture caused the cyanoacrylates to polymerize, making the chemicals incredibly sticky and extremely difficult to work with. They dismissed cyanoacrylates as a possible solution.

Six years later, Coover supervised a research group testing a list of hundreds of compounds to find a heat-resistant acrylate polymer for jet cockpit canopies at Kodak's chemical plant in Kingsport, Tennessee. One of his researchers, Dr. Fred Joyner, spread a film of ethyl cyanoacrylate—the 910th compound on the list—between two refractometer prisms to test the ocular qualities of the compound. Joyner discovered that he had inadvertently glued the prisms together, destroying an expensive laboratory machine.

Coover suddenly realized the potential for this sticky substance as an adhesive and urged his researchers to test the super-strength glue by gluing together everything in sight. In 1958, Kodak marketed the glue as Eastman 910, which later became known as Super Glue. Appearing as a guest on the television show *I've Got a Secret*, Coover used a single drop of Super Glue to adhere two steal cylinders together to raise the host of the show, Garry Moore, in the air. During the Vietnam War, Coover developed a Super Glue spray to seal wounds in battle so patients could be transferred safely to the hospital. Since then, scientists have developed an improved cyanoacrylate glue specifically for medical purposes.

WOOLY WILLY

I n the 1930s, brothers Don and Jim Herzog frequently went to work with their father, Ralph Herzog, the owner and founder of the Smethport Specialty Company, a toy factory in Smethport, Pennsylvania. The two boys loved watching idle factory workers use magnets to play with iron-ore shavings.

While attending a trade show in the 1940s, Don and Jim Herzog, then in their twenties, noticed a display on vacuum encasing. Realizing that this new technology would enable them to encase loose iron-ore shavings safely behind a plastic window, the Herzog brothers designed a chubby cartoon face with a

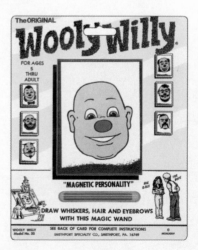

bald head and a red nose and launched Wooly Willy in 1955.

With the attached magnet, children and the young at heart could move around the iron-ore shavings to give Wooly Willy a head of hair, a moustache, a beard, a patch over his eye, or dark sunglasses. Should anyone's imagination need a kick-start, illustrations on the back of the package suggested nine disguises for Wooly Willy, including "Pete the Pirate" and "Dick the Dude."

The Herzog brothers quickly discovered that children nationwide shared their fascination with moving iron-ore fillings with a magnet. Sales of Wooly Willy skyrocketed, turning the toy into an American icon.

KLEENEX

n 1924, paper manufacturer Kimberly-Clark introduced Kleenex Kerchiefs as a disposable facial towel to remove makeup and cold cream. The following year, Chicago inventor Andrew Olsen designed Serv-a-Tissue, a pop-up tissue box that Kimberly-Clark soon produced for its Kleenex Kerchiefs. The first advertisement for Kleenex Kerchiefs appeared in the *Ladies Home Journal* in 1925 and touted the new product as "the new secret of keeping a pretty skin as used by famous movie stars." Two years later, Kleenex ads in women's magazines began featuring movie stars endorsing the disposable face towel.

Housewives soon discovered that their husbands were using

their Kleenex Kerchiefs as disposable handkerchiefs, and the subsequent letters of praise to Kimberly-Clark prompted the company to test-market the two possible uses for the product. In 1930, Kimberly-Clark offered consumers in Peoria, Illinois, two different coupons redeemable for a free box of the tissue. Sixty percent chose the offer describing the product as a disposable handkerchief rather than a face towel. That same year, Kimberly-Clark began promoting Kleenex tissue as a handkerchief substitute, and sales instantly doubled.

EUREKA DIAMOND

n 1866, fifteen-year-old Erasmus Jacobs picked up a small, attractive white stone on the banks of the Orange River on the De Kalk farm near Hopetown, South Africa. He put it in his pocket, brought it home, and played with the unusual stone for a month. One day while Jacobs played a game of "five stone" (similar to "jacks") with his family, neighboring farmer Schalk van Niekerk offered to buy the intriguing white stone. Jacobs's mother laughed at the offer and gave the stone to van Niekerk as a gift.

A few months later, van Niekerk showed the stone to his friend, John Robert O'Reilly, who suspected it might be a diamond. O'Reilly

sent the stone to the nearest geologist within a 200-mile radius—Dr. William Guybon Atherstone in Grahamstown. Atherstone identified the stone as a 21.25-carat rough diamond valued at 500 British pounds (approximately 73 U.S. dollars).

As equal partners, O'Reilly and van Niekerk sold the stone—dubbed the Eureka diamond (possibly by van Niekerk when he learned its true value)—to Sir Philip Wodehouse, governor of Cape Colony. Erasmus Jacobs never received any money for his discovery.

Oddly, the discovery of the Eureka diamond, the first authenticated diamond found in South Africa, did not spark the country's massive diamond mining industry. Instead, the 1869 discovery of the 83.5-carat Star of South Africa diamond ignited the nation's diamond rush.

TEFLON

On April 6, 1938, Dr. Roy J. Plunkett, a chemist working at the DuPont laboratory in Deepwater, New Jersey, opened a tank of gaseous tetrafluoroethylene to prepare a nontoxic refrigerant. No gas came out of the tank, which surprised Plunkett because the weight of the tank indicated it was full. Perplexed, Plunkett tested the valve to find out whether the gas had leaked from the tank. The valve was fine. So Plunkett sawed open the tank to examine the interior.

Inside the tank, Plunkett found an inexplicable waxy white powder. He realized that the molecules of the gaseous tetrafluoroethylene had somehow bonded with each other to form a solid polymer. No solvent would dissolve this slippery waxy white

powder. No acids or bases affected it. Heat would not melt it. Plunkett and his colleagues ultimately figured out how to produce "polytetrafluoroethylene," but the process was expensive. DuPont gave the compound the trade name Teflon and forgot about it.

A few months later, scientists developing the first atomic bomb needed gaskets made from a material that would withstand the corrosiveness of uranium hexafluoride. General Leslie R. Groves, having learned about the indestructible new compound from acquaintances that worked at DuPont, instructed the company to manufacture gaskets and valves from the slippery polymer. In tests, the Teflon components endured their exposure to uranium hexafluoride.

In 1960, DuPont introduced Teflon-coated frying pans and muffin tins. As one of the few substances that the human body does not reject, Teflon has been used to create artificial body parts such as aortas, corneas, bones, tendons, heart valves, and dentures. Teflon has also been used to insulate electrical wires and cables, provide the outer skin of space suits, and create the nose cones, heat shields, and fuel tanks of spacecrafts.

CERES

On January 1, 1801, Italian monk Giuseppe Piazzi, working in the observatory of Palermo on the island of Sicily to catalog known stars in the Taurus constellation, spotted a tiny point of light through the telescope. At first, he thought he had located a dim star

not recorded on his chart, but when he checked the star the following night, its position had changed dramatically, indicating that Piazzi was observing something other than a star. At first, Piazzi thought he had discovered a comet, until he considered its slow, uniform movement and the lack of dust and gas.

Piazzi wrote to a number of his colleagues to inform them of his findings. Without ever seeing the object, Johann Bode, director of the Berlin Observatory, concluded that Piazzi had found "the missing planet" that seventeenth century German astronomer Johannes Kepler believed existed in the large gap between the orbits of Mars and Jupiter. Piazzi named the object Ceres after the Roman goddess of agriculture.

In 1802, German-born British astronomer William Herschel coined the word *asteroid* to describe Ceres—due to its small size. Scientists have since discovered millions of asteroids in the asteroid belt between Mars and Jupiter. In 2006, the International Astronomical Union reclassified Ceres, a sphere with a diameter of roughly 600 miles, as a dwarf planet.

WATERMARKS

I n 1282, a small piece of wire got caught in the paper press being used at the Fabriano Paper Mill in Fabriano, Italy, a town renowned for its papermaking factories and the high-quality paper produced there. The piece of wire made a line in the finished paper that could be seen only by holding the paper up to the light. The papermakers realized that a design made from wire could be used to create a decorative watermark on the paper during the papermaking process, which could also be used on banknotes, stamps, and other government documents to thwart counterfeiters.

From that moment on, each paper mill branded its paper with its own distinctive watermark consisting of a drawing or a letter to identify its products. For centuries, all Italian banknotes, and those of many other European countries, were printed at Fabriano. Today, Fabriano is home to the Paper and Watermark Museum.

CHAMPAGNE

I n 1668, Benedictine monk Pierre Pérignon arrived at the Abbey of Hautvillers near the town of Épernay (in the Champagne region of France) to serve as cellar master and winemaker. His superiors instructed him to get rid of the irritating fizz in the wine, which was a sign of poor winemaking.

The bubbles in the wine resulted from the region's cold climate and short growing season. Farmers harvested grapes late in the year, due to necessity. When the grapes were pressed into grape juice, the yeasts present on the grape skins did not have enough time to convert all of the sugar in the juice into alcohol because the cold winter temperatures stopped

the fermentation process. The winemakers bottled the wine, and when the spring arrived, the warm temperatures reawakened the fermentation process, which continued inside the sealed bottle. The refermentation produced carbon dioxide which, trapped in the bottle, carbonated the wine, frequently causing the bottle to explode.

During his forty-seven years at the Abbey of Hautvillers, Dom Pérignon tried tirelessly to prevent bubbles from forming in his wines, but he failed miserably. He did, however, develop the technique used to press red wine grapes to yield white wine, master the art of blending the juice of different grapes, and improve clarification techniques to produce a brighter wine than had ever been produced before. To prevent the bottles from exploding, he used stronger bottles developed by the English and sealed them closed with Spanish cork rather than the wood and oil-soaked hemp stoppers commonly used in his day. Although he failed to eliminate the bubbles, Dom Pérignon initiated and instituted the basic principles still used today to make champagne—and his sparkling white wine became the libation of choice by the English and French royalty and aristocracy.

MATCHES

I n 1827, pharmacist John Walker in Stockton-on-Tees, England, finished stirring a pot of chemicals—antimony sulfide, potassium chlorate, gum, and starch—and noticed that a dried lump of the mixture had adhered to the end of his stirring stick. When he tried to scrape

the lump off the end of the stick by dragging it across the floor, the substance burst into flame. Realizing that he had accidentally invented the strikeable match, Walker dipped three-inch cardboard sticks into the mixture and packaged his "friction lights" in a round "pillar-box" with a small piece of folded sandpaper to be used as the striking surface. He sold his first box of matches on April 12, 1827.

Walker refused to patent his discovery, freely demonstrating the matches to anyone interested.

Samuel Jones from London swiftly copied the idea, producing "Lucifer" matches in a small cardboard box, giving birth to the modern-day matchbox. (Lucifers were composed of a glass vial of sulfuric acid wrapped in paper, which, when crushed, would ignite the paper.) In 1855, Swedish match factory owner Johan Edvard Lundström developed the first safety match using red phosphorous. Today, over 500 billion matches are used each year, with about 200 billion from matchbooks, making the phrase "close cover before striking" the most printed expression in the English language.

ANNETTE FUNICELLO

During Easter week in 1955, 12-year-old Annette Funicello, the daughter of an automobile mechanic, danced ballet in "Swan Lake" at a local school recital at the Burbank Starlight Bowl in California. In the audience happened to be Walt Disney, whose friend Leo Damiani was conducting the orchestra. At the time, Disney was looking for amateurs rather than professional child actors to play the role of Mouseketeers in his new children's television show, *The Mickey Mouse Club*.

When Annette pirouetted onto the stage as the Swan Queen, Disney recognized her "star quality." The next day, Disney studio executives called dance teacher Al Gilbert to find out who the girl was and invite her to audition. Disney chose her as the last of the twenty-four original Mouseketeers for *The Mickey Mouse Club*.

With her timeless, classic beauty and charming innocence, Annette became the most beloved Mouseketeer and "America's sweetheart." During the first season of the show, she received more than 6,000 fan letters a month. To capitalize on her popularity, Disney marketed Annette lunchboxes, dolls, mystery novels, and other ancillary products. When *The Mickey Mouse Club* ended in 1958, Disney offered Funicello a studio contract and gave her starring roles in the movies *The Shaggy Dog* and *Babes in Toyland*. Beginning in 1963, with Disney's consent, Annette costarred with Frankie Avalon in eight beach movies, including *Beach Blanket Bingo* and *How to Stuff a Wild Bikini*.

TEMPLO MAYOR

On February 21, 1978, three electrical workers began digging a trench beneath the streets of Mexico City near the capitol's spacious Zocalo and National Cathedral to install underground electric cables. They struck an immense, eight-ton stone disk.

The workers recognized the carvings on the disk as images of dismembered and decapitated parts of the Aztec moon goddess, Coyolxauhqui, who had been slain by her brother, the war god Huitzilopochtli. Archaeologists from the National Anthropology and History Institute investigated and immediately knew they had found the ruins of the Aztec Templo Mayor of

Tenochtitlan, built in 1325 and buried beneath Mexico City for four centuries.

In 1521, Spanish conquistadors demolished the Templo Mayor, a pyramid rising ninety feet with a pair of summit temples dedicated to Huitzilopochtli and the rain god Tlaloc. The Mexican government decided to demolish the surrounding colonial buildings and excavate Templo Mayor. Since then, archaeologists have uncovered hundreds of ceremonial offerings, including the skeletons of two eagles, sacrificial knives, and the skulls of thirty-four children whom the Aztecs had sacrificed to Tlaloc. These artifacts, along with the stone disk of Coyolxauhqui, can be visited at the Museo del Templo Mayor in Mexico City.

MOLECULAR STRUCTURE

Before 1865, chemists had no idea what chemicals looked like on the molecular level. Seven years earlier, German chemist Friedrich August Kekulé, riding aboard a London city bus late at night, fell asleep and dreamt of atoms. "The atoms were gamboling before my eyes," he recalled in an 1890 speech in Berlin. He saw two small atoms unite to form a pair, a large atom embrace the two smaller atoms, larger atoms capture three or four smaller atoms, and atoms forming a chain. Based on this dream, Kekulé formed the basis of his Structural Theory, noting that certain carbon atoms could link together in chains, with hydrogen atoms or other atoms connected to them.

In 1865, Kekulé went to Ghent, Belgium, to work as a chemistry professor. One night, he fell asleep in a chair by the fireplace in his study and dreamt of a long chain of molecules "all twining and twisting in snake-like motion." In his dream, "one of the snakes had seized hold of its own tail, and the form whirled mockingly before my eyes." Kekulé awoke and spent the rest of the night developing his theory that the six carbon atoms in the chemical benzene formed a ring (like the snake biting its own tail) with one hydrogen atom attached to each carbon atom—becoming the first person to suggest a suitable molecular structure for benzene, originating the structure theory of organic chemistry.

MILK-BONE DOG BISCUITS

n the late 1800s, the owner of a London butcher shop that also made baked goods, tried to create a new recipe for tea biscuits to sell to his customers. Deciding that his new batch of biscuits tasted awful, he tossed one to his dog, who quickly gobbled up the treat, inspiring the butcher with a new idea. Dog owners throughout the city were soon clamoring to buy this new canine treat now shaped like a bone and packaged specifically for dog owners.

In 1908, Manhattan baker F. H. Bennett bought the recipe from the butcher, and the F. H. Bennett Biscuit Co. was soon marketing the dog biscuit under the brand name Malatoid, receiving a trademark in 1911.

Since milk was a primary ingredient in the biscuit, the company changed the name to Milk-Bone in 1915.

In 1931, the Nabisco Biscuit Company acquired Milk-Bone dog biscuits, the only dog biscuit commercially available to the public for fifty years. Initially, Nabisco advertised the treat strictly as an indulgence for dogs. Eventually, the company began to capitalize on the fact that Milk-Bone biscuits clean a dog's teeth, improve a dog's breath, and nutritionally supplement a dog's regular diet. Now, more than one hundred years later, the brand, owned by Del Monte Foods, is the best-selling dog treat in the world.

MICROWAVE OVEN

Shortly after World War II, navy veteran and self-taught electrical engineer Percy Spencer was touring a laboratory at the Raytheon Company where he worked in Waltham, Massachusetts. He stopped in front of a magnetron, an electron tube that generates high-frequency radio waves to power a radar set. Suddenly, Spencer noticed that the chocolate bar in his pocket had begun to melt. Intrigued, he held a bag of popcorn

kernels next to the magnetron, only to discover that the radio waves popped the kernels into popcorn. The following day, Spencer placed an egg in a pot and held it near the magnetron. The egg exploded. Spencer quickly realized that the microwaves had cooked the egg from the inside out, and the resulting pressure had caused the shell to burst.

In 1945, Spencer used the magnetron—a device invented in 1940 by Sir John Randall and Dr. H. A. Boot at Birmingham University to create radar to help England fight the Nazis—to develop the first microwave oven, weighing 750 pounds and standing five feet six inches tall. Two years later, Raytheon marketed the Radarange microwave oven (named by an employee in a company contest) to restaurants, passenger railroad dining cars, and cruise ships. Unfortunately, the original microwave oven could not brown meat and left French fries white and limp. Twenty years later, engineers at Raytheon improved the microwave oven, and the company, having acquired Amana Refrigeration in 1965, began marketing Radarange microwave ovens to consumers.

In 1975, Americans bought more microwave ovens than gas ranges. Today, there are over 200 million microwave ovens in use throughout the world.

PENICILLIN

I n November 1921, Dr. Alexander Fleming suffered a cold but continued working in the laboratory at St. Mary's Hospital in London. A drop of mucus from his runny nose accidentally dripped into a petri dish and dissolved some colonies of bacteria. Fleming had discovered lysozyme, an antibacterial enzyme contained in tears, nasal mucus, and saliva. The discovery launched Fleming on a search for stronger antibacterial substances.

In the summer of 1928, Fleming used a microscope to examine cultures of *Staphylococcus aureus* grown in petri dishes to study the virulence of the bacteria. In July, he went on vacation, leaving forty to fifty petri dishes piled on his laboratory bench.

Upon his return on September 3, Fleming noticed in one of the petri dishes a clear area encircling a spot where a spore of airborne mold had accidentally fallen into the staphylococcus culture and germinated. Based on his experience with lysozyme, Fleming realized that the mold emitted a substance that dissolved the bacteria.

That mold turned out to be *Penicillium notatum*, a rare organism being cultivated in the mycology laboratory on the floor below Fleming's laboratory. The spore had apparently wafted upstairs and landed on one of Fleming's petri dishes immediately after he had implanted the agar with staphylococci. Had the spore landed later, the blooming bacteria would have prevented the penicillium from multiplying.

Fleming extracted a bright yellow fluid from the mold and discovered that his "mold juice" (which he named *penicillin*) killed the bacteria responsible for staphylococci infections, streptococcal infections, pneumonia, meningitis, gonorrhea, and diphtheria—without harming the human body. Nearly a decade later, researchers at Oxford University— pathologist Howard W. Florey and biochemist Ernst Boris Chain—purified and concentrated penicillin, turning it into a lifesaving drug.

TAUNG CHILD

n 1924, E. G. Izod, a director of Rand Mines Limited, visited the Buxton Limeworks—a quarry near Taung, South Africa (270 miles southwest of Johannesburg). Workers in the quarry frequently unearthed fossils of

baboons from the limestone, and the manager of the mining company gave a fossil of a baboon cranium to Izod as a souvenir. In turn, Izod gave the skull to his son Pat, a student at the University of Witwatersrand in South Africa, who displayed it on his mantel.

One of Pat's classmates, Josephine Salmons, noticed the skull and borrowed it to show to her anatomy professor, 32-year-old Raymond Dart, who recognized the relic as a baboon fossil. Professor Dart asked his colleague Robert B. Young, a professor of geology at the university, to use his connections with the mining company at the Buxton Limeworks to have any similar crania and skulls found in the mines shipped to him.

In the fall, Mr. M. de Bruyn, the quarry-master at the Buxton Limeworks spotted a skull in the rubble after a blast and, noting that it looked different from the now familiar baboon skulls, brought it to the mining office. When Professor Young visited the Buxton Limeworks in November, the mine manager showed the specimen to him. Young brought the fossil back to Dart.

After cleaning the limestone from the fossil, Dart identified the skull as belonging to an ancient adolescent child more than a million years old, proposed that the fossil represented an extinct missing link between humans and apes, and named it *Australopithecus africanus*. Based on the shape of the skull, Dart deduced in the pages of the esteemed publication *Nature* in 1925 that the Taung child walked upright, the first evidence of a bipedal human—a claim later corroborated by eminent archaeologists.

AVON

n the 1880s, door-to-door book salesman David McConnell gave small bottles of homemade perfume as "door openers" to New England housewives who listened to his sales pitch. McConnell quickly realized that his female customers were far more interested in the perfume than the books. He also noticed that many of the women, struggling to make ends meet, possessed natural sales skills to which other women would easily relate, such as an innate ability to add a personal and empathetic touch to the exchange.

In 1886, McConnell created the California Perfume Company, hiring women to sell door-to-door and giving them the opportunity to create and manage their own businesses. Within thirteen years, McConnell had more than 5,000 sales representatives.

Renamed "Avon" in 1939 after the Avon River in England, the company became the world's largest cosmetics enterprise. In the 1960s, Avon became a household word—thanks to the prevalence of "Avon Ladies" and television commercials in which a doorbell rings, followed by the catchphrase, "Avon calling."

INSULIN

n 1889, German scientists Joseph von Mering and Oscar Minkowski, working at the University of Strasbourg, removed the pancreas from a dog to study how the canine's digestive process functioned without the organ. A few days later, a laboratory assistant noticed flies swarming around a puddle of the dog's urine. Perplexed, the two scientists analyzed the urine and discovered an abundance of sugar.

Aware that sugar in urine generally indicates diabetes, von Mering and Minkowski realized that removing the pancreas from the dog had rendered the animal diabetic. In due time, they proved that the pancreas secretes a substance that helps

the body metabolize sugar and the lack of this secretion results in diabetes.

In 1921, medical doctor Frederick G. Banting and medical student Charles H. Best, working at the University of Toronto in Canada, extracted the secretion from the pancreases of dogs. They injected the extracts into dogs whose pancreases had been removed and then tested the urine. The urine proved free of sugar, and the blood-sugar levels of the dogs returned to normal.

Professor John J. R. Macleod, whose laboratory Banting and Best were using, improved the method for extracting the substance, standardized its dosage, and suggested that the secretion be named *insulin* (after the fact that insular cells in the pancreas produced it). In 1922, Banting and Macleod tested purified insulin from bovine pancreases on human diabetics—relieving the symptoms of diabetes. The next year, Banting and Macleod received the Noble Prize in physiology for having isolated insulin and developing clinical ways to use it to control diabetes.

ICE-CREAM CONE

At the 1904 World's Fair in St. Louis, Missouri, twenty-year-old Syrian immigrant Ernest Hamwi operated a concession stand and sold zalabia, a thin, crisp, wafer-like pasty baked on a flat waffle iron and served with sugar or other sweets—a popular treat in Middle Eastern countries. One hot summer day, Arnold Fornachou, the French-American ice-cream vendor working next to Hamwi, ran out of bowls to serve his confection. Hamwi cleverly rolled one of his thin waffles into the shape of a cone, let it cool, and handed the hardened cone to Fornachou to fill with ice cream, giving birth to the ice-cream cone.

Sales for both Fornachou and Hamwi boomed, and several newspapers reported that

"World's Fair cornucopias" became a common sight at the exhibition. Hamwi's invention, being edible, eliminated the litter problem caused by paper bowls, required no implements to eat, and enabled the consumer to lick rather than gobble the ice cream, prolonging the pleasure.

For years afterward, ice-cream cone vendors would use a waffle iron to make a waffle and then roll it into a cone. In 1910, Fred Bruckmann of Portland, Oregon, developed a machine that automatically poured batter into a moving mold and trimmed the resulting cone—creating the first automated ice-cream cone.

BRA

I n the winter of 1913, 21-year-old socialite Mary Phelps Jacob (who later changed her name to Caresse Crosby) attended her New York debutante ball wearing a clumsy and constricting corset-like contraption under her dress. Soon afterward, while dressing for another dance, she grew distressed by what she later called in her autobiography, *The Passionate Years*, the "boxlike armor of whalebone and pink cordage" protruding above the neck of her dress. Crosby summoned her personal maid and refused to wear the cumbersome undergarment again. "Bring me two of my pocket handkerchiefs," she recalled saying, "and some pink ribbon . . . And bring the needle and thread and some pins."

After the dance, her girlfriends insisted upon knowing how Crosby had moved about so freely, creating unforeseen demand for the newly devised bra. In 1914, Crosby secured a patent for "the backless brassiere." After setting up a factory and going into business manufacturing bras, Crosby sold her company and design to the Warner Brothers Corset Company of Connecticut for a mere $1,500. Over the next thirty years, the Warner Brothers Corset Company earned a purported $15 million in bra sales.

In 1916, Manhattan dress shop owner William Rosenthal came up the idea of fashioning brassieres by cup size. His wife, Ida, a Russian immigrant and seamstress, designed and sewed the prototype. In 1925, when demand for the new support bra exceeded their expectations, the Rosenthals and their friend, Enid Bisset, formed a company that would eventually become known as Maidenform.

ELECTRIC WELDING

One evening in 1876, British-born Elihu Thomson, a science professor at Central High School in Philadelphia, demonstrated various forms of electricity during a routine physics lecture at the nearby Franklin Institute. While discharging the electricity from several Leyden jars connected in series through a large high-tension jump spark coil, Thomson held the ends of the two primary wires in contact with each other to complete the circuit. Afterward, Thomson could not pull the two wires apart. Upon closer examination, he realized that the heat produced by the electrical current had fused the copper wires together. Thomson had discovered electric welding.

Thomson immediately built an electrical welding

machine, receiving a patent for his invention in 1886. Electric welding changed the face of welding, allowing welders to fuse metals together without the more intricate use of a torch. Thomson became one of the most prolific inventors in American history and joined Thomas Edison to form General Electric.

RUBY FALLS

n 1905, the Southern Railroad Company began building a railway tunnel through portions of Lookout Mountain near Chattanooga, Tennessee, and permanently sealed off the natural entrance to Lookout Mountain Cave, closing it to the public. Eighteen years later, chemist and local cave enthusiast Leo Lambert, having explored Lookout Mountain Cave prior to its closure, formed a company to reopen the cave as a tourist attraction. Lambert  planned to drill an elevator shaft from another point on the mountain to access the cave.

On December 28, 1928, while excavating the elevator shaft, a worker operating a jackhammer discovered a void in the rock 160 feet above the cave and felt a gush of air. Further inspection revealed a passageway eighteen inches tall and five feet wide. Lambert and a small crew crawled through this opening and found, much to their astonishment, another cave containing a magnificent 145-foot-tall underground waterfall.

On his next exploration into the cave, Lambert took his wife Ruby, and while gazing at the waterfall, named it "Ruby Falls" in her honor. Lambert developed both Lookout Mountain Cave and the newly discovered Ruby Falls Cave into tourist attractions. The water from Ruby Falls contains large quantities of magnesium from the layers of rock, making it a natural laxative (although no one has determined the proper dosage).

TEDDY BEARS

n 1902, President Theodore Roosevelt traveled south to negotiate a border dispute between the states of Mississippi and Louisiana. During a break from the negotiations, Roosevelt accepted an invitation to join a hunting expedition in Smedes, Mississippi. After ten days of hunting, Roosevelt failed to spot a single bear. His hosts, hoping to please the president, searched the woods, found a small bear cub, tethered it to a tree outside Roosevelt's tent, and cried "Bear!" to beckon the president. Roosevelt emerged from his tent, took one look at the frightened cub, and refused to kill such a young animal.

Newspapers reported the event. In the *Washington Star*, political cartoonist Clifford K. Berryman drew a caricature of Roosevelt with his hand upraised, refusing to shoot the cuddly bear cub. The caption read, "Drawing the Line in Mississippi," cleverly referring to the unresolved border dispute.

Inspired by the cartoon, Brooklyn toy-store owner Morris Michtom, a 32-year-old Russian immigrant, made a stuffed bear cub and displayed it alongside the political cartoon in his store window to generate attention. When customers wanted to buy their own "Teddy's Bear," Michtom began making them, founding the Ideal Toy Company.

Meanwhile in Germany, stuffed toy maker Margarete Steiff, similarly inspired by Berryman's political cartoon, created her own stuffed bear toy. In 1906, guests at a White House wedding reception for Roosevelt's daughter discovered tables decorated with Steiff bears dressed as hunters and fishermen as a tribute to the president's love for the outdoors. While mulling over the possible breed of the animals, a wedding guest cleverly labeled them "Teddy Bears."

WINDOVER ARCHAEOLOGICAL SITE

n 1982, backhoe operator Steve Vanderjagt, draining a
pond in Titusville, Florida, to build a road for a new
upscale housing development called Windover Farms,
noticed what looked like a shiny rock in the bucket of his
machine. Mindful that rocks are scarce on the central
coast of Florida, Vanderjagt got out of his backhoe to
examine the rock, which turned out to be a human skull.

Suspecting murder, the developers called the
police, but the sheriff and county medical examiner
determined that the skulls had been buried long ago.
Developers Jack Eckerd and Jim Swann ceased construction
and summoned archaeologists from Florida State
University. Radiocarbon dating showed the bones to be
roughly 7,000 years old. Eckerd and Swann redesigned

the housing development and designated the pond as the Windover Archaeological Site.

Archaeologists have found the remains of 168 skeletons, including brain tissue, remarkably preserved due to the preservative effect of the pond's peat-bottom. The pond—designated a United States National Historic Landmark in 1987—represents one of the largest archaeological finds from the Archaic period in the Americas.

MILK DUDS

n 1926, candy manufacturer F. Hoffman & Company in Chicago attempted to develop a perfectly round, chocolate-covered caramel morsel made with a large amount of milk. The machines, however, produced lopsided balls. Still, the deformed chocolate "duds" tasted wonderful, so the company decided to market the misshapen morsels under the name Milk Duds.

In 1928, Milton J. Holloway took over F. Hoffman & Company, and under his leadership, sales of Milk Duds went through the roof. Milk Duds chocolate-covered caramels became a staple of movie theater candy counters. After Holloway sold the company in 1960, several companies bought and sold the Milk Duds brand, which is now owned by the

Hershey Company. The factory produces one million of the marble-sized candies every 2 hours and 37 minutes. The enduring popularity of Milk Duds makes the idea of promoting a defect as an attribute, considered risky at the time, seem ingenious in retrospect.

POLYETHYLENE

n March 1933, researcher R. O. Gibson, a chemist at Imperial Chemical Industries (ICI) in Northwich, England, tested the reaction between ethylene gas and benzaldehyde under high pressure. Afterward, he discovered that the walls of the reaction vessel were coated with a thin layer of a white, waxy solid, which his colleagues identified as polyethylene. When he repeated the experiment with ethylene gas alone, the white, waxy solid failed to materialize.

In December 1935, after the company designed and built better high-pressure equipment, scientists continued testing the effect of high pressure on ethylene gas alone. When the temperature in the reaction vessel reached 180 degrees centigrade, the pressure suddenly dropped dramatically, due to a leak in the apparatus, prompting the scientists to add more ethylene gas. The experiment produced eight grams of white powder.

After months of investigation, the research team determined that the experiment had produced polyethylene due to the leak, which had allowed a small amount of oxygen to enter the chamber. The fresh infusion of ethylene then contained just the right amount of oxygen to force the ethylene molecules to bond together. Oddly, the scientists at ICI could not envision any practical use for polyethylene.

In 1939, J. N. Dean of the British Telegraph Construction and Maintenance Company happened to hear about the new polymer and, needing a water-resistant material to insulate the underwater telegraph and telephone cables that his company was about to produce, commissioned ICI to produce enough polyethylene to coat one nautical mile of cable. Since then, polyethylene has been used to insulate flexible cable for radar equipment, replace cellophane, and create the ubiquitous plastic garbage bag.

BIRTH CONTROL PILL

n 1953, biologist Gregory Pincus, recruited by activist Margaret Sanger and sponsored by heiress Katherine McCormick to create an oral contraceptive, approached the pharmaceutical company G. D. Searle in Skokie, Illinois, to fund his research. Not wishing to get involved in the controversial area of birth control, tangle with the restrictive birth control laws in thirty states, or provoke a boycott from American Catholics (who comprised 25 percent of the population), Searle declined. Also, company

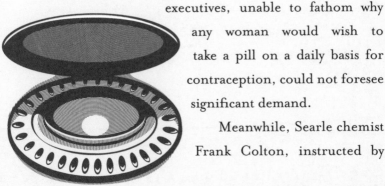

executives, unable to fathom why any woman would wish to take a pill on a daily basis for contraception, could not foresee significant demand.

Meanwhile, Searle chemist Frank Colton, instructed by

the company to find more uses for steroids, had developed an orally effective synthetic progesterone compound to treat women suffering from a variety of gynecological disorders. The company discovered that Colton's drug, called norethynodrel, also impeded ovulation.

Gregory Pincus no longer needed to create the contraceptive drug. He merely needed to test it. Reluctant to fund the research directly, Searle gave samples of norethynodrel to Pincus for his trials. In 1956, Pincus discovered that Searle had sent him pills contaminated with a minuscule amount of synthetic estrogen. However, his trials revealed that the estrogen reduced some of the original pill's side effects.

In 1957, Searle released the pill under the brand name Enovid as a treatment for gynecological disorders. When women across America started using the pill for its contraceptive effect, Searle recognized the drug's commercial potential. Finally, in 1960, the U.S. Food and Drug Administration approved the pill for contraceptive use, and within two years, 1.2 million women were taking it daily, making it Searle's best-selling product.

COBB SALAD

n 1937, Robert Cobb, owner of the Brown Derby, the renowned Hollywood restaurant shaped like a hat and decorated with celebrity caricatures on the walls, wanted a midnight snack before closing up shop. Uninterested in the Derby's standard fare (hamburgers, hot dogs, chili, and grilled cheese sandwiches), he threw together a salad from ingredients he found in the kitchen: chopped chicken breast, iceberg lettuce, romaine, avocado, hard-boiled eggs, watercress, chicory, chives, tomatoes, bacon, black olives, Roquefort cheese, and vinaigrette dressing.

As Cobb ate his improvised salad, Sid Grauman (owner of Hollywood's Chinese Theatre) entered the restaurant after a film preview. Intrigued by Cobb's creation, Grauman ordered a plate of Cobb's salad for himself. Soon regular customers—including Hollywood mogul Jack Warner and movie stars Humphrey Bogart and Frank Sinatra—began ordering the off-menu salad.

Eventually, Cobb added the popular salad, named after himself, to the Brown Derby menu. The Cobb salad quickly became an American classic.

NUCLEAR FISSION

n 1934, two years after English physicist James Chadwick discovered the neutron, Italian physicist Enrico Fermi in Rome found that bombarding almost any element with neutrons transformed the nucleus of the element and produced new radioactive elements.

Five years later, German chemists Otto Hahn and Fritz Strassmann, working at the Kaiser Wilhelm Institute of Chemistry at Berlin-Dahlen, bombarded solutions of uranium salts with neutrons in the hope of creating an element heavier than uranium. Through chemical analysis, they determined that the bombardment had produced barium, an element whose atoms are about half the size of

uranium atoms. Hahn wrote to his former colleague Lise Meitner, a Jewish physicist who had fled to Sweden to escape Nazi Germany, describing the perplexing results that he and Strassmann had achieved and pleading for an explanation.

Meitner and her nephew Otto Frisch, a physicist visiting from Denmark, deduced that a uranium nucleus, having captured a neutron, had split into two roughly equal parts, one of which was barium. Frisch named the process "fission" after the process by which a cell divides itself in two.

FINGERPRINTING

lthough Francis Galton devised a scientific system for classifying fingerprints in 1892, detecting the incriminating marks remained problematic.

In 1977, Fuseo Matsumur, a hair and fiber expert at the police crime laboratory in Saga, Japan, used superglue to adhere trace evidence on a glass slide to examine under a microscope. Matsumur suddenly noticed his fingerprint developing on the slide. Intrigued, he showed the slide to

his colleague, fingerprint examiner Masato Soba, who experimented with his own fingerprints and eventually developed a technique for detecting fingerprints using superglue.

A fingerprint leaves invisible trace elements of amino acids, fatty acids, and proteins on smooth surfaces.

The fumes from superglue (cyanoacrylate) condense on oils in the fingerprints, harden, and turn the prints white and indelible. Investigators simply set the item to be tested in a fish tank, placed a few drops of cyanoacrylate in a container, and waited for the cyanoacrylate vapor to reveal the fingerprints.

In 1979, the National Police Agency of Japan demonstrated the superglue-fuming method for fingerprint examiners from the U.S. Army Crime Laboratory, who then instituted the procedure in the United States.

"You can just leave plain superglue in a little container for anywhere from thirty-six hours to thirty days, and any prints that are there will develop," Super Glue Corp.'s operations manager Carol Donnelly told *Popular Science* in 1985. "But no one wants to wait for thirty days." Since then, scientists have accelerated the process by adding a catalyst to the cyanoacrylate to speed the fuming process, a technique now used in most crime labs around the world.

BISKUPIN VILLAGE

n 1933, Walenty Szwajcer, a young teacher on a field trip with his class in Poland, noticed wooden stakes sticking up near the side of Biskupinskie Lake. He shared his observation with the museum in the nearby city of Poznań.

Several months later, archaeologist Józef Kostrzewski, a professor at the University of Poznań, investigated the site and initiated the largest excavation project in Polish history, unearthing the ancient village of Biskupin, which had been built on an island in the middle of the lake around

737 B.C.E. The village, constructed from nearly 1,200 oak trees cut down from the nearby forest and transported to the island, covered some six acres. The people of the Lusatian culture had built the fortified structure, composed of more than one hundred houses and surrounded by walls and an embankment of logs, to protect themselves from aggressive Germanic neighbors. Archaeologists found weapons, tools, and pottery.

The inhabitants abandoned the village in the fifth century B.C.E. for unknown reasons. The site gradually disappeared under the rising waters of the lake. In the 1930s, dredging of the rivers in the area lowered the water level of the lake, causing the village to resurface.

"RAIN"

Typically, when the Beatles worked on a song in the studio, they'd take a rough mix of the song home on a reel-to-reel tape. Halfway through recording the song "Rain" on April 14, 1966, John Lennon asked for a copy of the rough mix. The engineer recorded a copy of the tape onto a small reel and, without rewinding it, placed it in a box and handed it to Lennon. "I took the tracks home to see what gimmicks I  could add, because the song wasn't quite right," recalled Lennon in a 1969 interview. When he arrived home, he thread the tape onto his reel-to-reel machine, not realizing he needed to rewind the tape first, and inadvertently played it backward.

"I . . . stuck the tape on . . . backwards and played 'Rain' and it came out backwards," recalled Lennon in *The Beatles: Off the Record*, " . . . and I was thinking, 'Wow, this is fantastic.' So, the next day I went in and said, 'What about the end of the song? Why don't we have the whole song again, you know, backwards?'"

The Beatles ended up inserting a coda with a half-minute of the vocal track ("When the rain comes . . . ") and guitar accompaniment played backward, marking the first time any musical group had used a backward recording in one of their songs. (George Harrison figured out the notes he needed to play forward to achieve the desired result backward.)

"You can hear it at the end," said Lennon. "It sounds as if I'm singing Indian."

THERMOSTATIC SWITCH

n 1907, fifteen-year-old John Alby Spencer, working in a clothespin mill in northern Maine, was assigned to keep the steam boiler that powered the machinery burning at a constant temperature by adding wood whenever necessary. The boiler burned the waste chips and wood shavings so quickly that Spencer barely had time to perform his other duties before he had to race back to look into the firebox to see if the boiler needed more fuel. Spencer noticed that whenever the fire started to burn very hot, he would hear a sharp, metallic pop. When the fire began to cool down, he would hear the same noise.

One day, Spencer discovered the source of the noise. The expansion and contraction of the metal caused the round clean-out door at the top of the boiler to belly out into a convex shape when the fire heated and snap back into a concave shape when the fire cooled. Realizing that he could use this phenomenon as an alarm system, Spencer merely listened for the loud popping sound made when the round door bulged out, signaling him to add more wood to the furnace.

Ten years later, Spencer applied that knowledge to craft a disk that could be calibrated to snap at desired temperature settings—for use as a thermostat. He welded together a disk of nickel steel (with a slow rate of expansion under heat) and a disk of Monel metal (with a fast rate of expansion) in such a way that the combination would be convex at a given temperature but would snap back when the temperature rose to a predetermined point. (In a thermostat, the center of the disk rests in contact against an electrical terminal, completing an electrical circuit. When the temperature rises beyond a certain point, the disk snaps back, breaking the circuit.) Today, Spencer's thermostatic switch is used in countless electrical appliances, including water heaters and toasters.

EX-LAX

n the early 1900s, pestilence destroyed many vineyards in Hungary. Unscrupulous vintners began pressing grapes a second time to squeeze more wine from their harvest, but doing so created an inferior acidic wine. To combat this practice, government inspectors began adding a few drops of phenolphthalein, a seemingly innocuous chemical agent, to the white wines to test the acidity. The chemical would turn an acidic white wine a pinkish-purple color. A diarrhea epidemic promptly ensued. Phenolphthalein turned out to have a laxative effect, and government inspectors ceased adding phenolphthalein to test the wines.

Several years later, Hungarian pharmacist Max Kiss immigrated to Brooklyn, New York, and opened a pharmacy. When local mothers complained about harsh, bitter-tasting laxatives like castor oil, Kiss recalled the effects of phenolphthalein and decided to mask the taste with chocolate. One evening in 1905, he teamed up with one of his neighbors, a foreman in a chocolate factory, mixed a small amount of phenolphthalein into some melted chocolate, and dripped it onto wax paper to cool, giving birth to a new product, which he dubbed Ex-Lax, an abbreviation for "excellent laxative."

Marketed as "the chocolate laxative," Ex-Lax became one of the best-selling laxatives in the United States. The phenolphthalein in Ex-Lax was replaced in 1997 with a natural laxative derived from the senna plant—in anticipation of the U.S. Food and Drug Administration's 1999 ban on phenolphthalein in over-the-counter laxatives due to concerns of possible carcinogenicity.

AURIGNAC CAVE

n 1852, a road worker named Jean-Baptiste Bonnemaison chased after a rabbit that suddenly disappeared into a hole near the town of Aurignac in southwestern France. Reaching his hand into what he thought was a rabbit

burrow, he pulled out a human bone—much to his astonishment. His curiosity piqued, Bonnemaison explored the hole further, pushed aside a slab of rock, and discovered the entrance to a cave, which contained human skeletons, bones of animals, and primitive paintings on the walls.

The mayor of Aurignac buried the human remains in the parish cemetery, and within eight years, the townspeople forgot the precise location of the buried bodies.

In 1860, French paleontologist Édouard Lartet examined the cave, discovered prehistoric tools and the bones of extinct animals eaten by man (including bear, lion, mammoth, elk, and reindeer). He theorized that the cave was the site of successive burials accompanied by funeral feasts. The cave paintings, dating back to 40,000 B.C.E. during the Paleolithic age, depict men hunting bison and tigers, catching fish, and climbing trees to obtain honey and gather fruits and nuts.

VACUUM CLEANER

At an exhibition at London's Empire Music Hall in 1898, aspiring inventor H. Cecil Booth watched an inventor demonstrate his new "dust-removing" machine. The contraption blew compressed air into a carpet in the futile hope of sending the dirt and dust flying back up into an attached metal box.

Upon learning that no inventor had succeeded in devising a machine that sucked up dust and dirt, Booth realized that the solution lay in finding the proper material to use as a filtering bag to trap the dirt and dust particles while allowing air to pass through. He tested different kinds of fabrics by placing each one over his lips, lying on the floor, and sucking the carpet with his mouth—eventually happening upon a tightly woven cloth handkerchief that filtered the dust perfectly.

In 1901, Booth patented his suction cleaner—a machine as large as a contemporary refrigerator that had to be rolled on a dolly by one person while a second person used an attached flexible hose to vacuum up dirt and dust. The vacuum cleaner, extracting germ-carrying dust from carpets and upholstered furniture, vastly improved sanitation and health.

In 1907, James Murray Spangler, a janitor working in a department store in Canton, Ohio, experienced fierce allergic reactions to the dust stirred up by the mechanical sweeper he used. Desperate to keep his job and determined to end his plight, Spangler decided to invent his own "dustless cleaning machine." He attached the motor from an old electric fan to a soap box, sealed the cracks with adhesive tape, and attached a pillow case as a dust bag. The following year, he received a patent for his invention and borrowed money from friends to found the Electric Suction Sweeper Company.

KOOL-AID

I n 1914, 25-year-old Edwin Perkins of Hendley, Nebraska—having concocted flavoring extracts and perfumes, published a weekly newspaper, and served as postmaster—set up a mail-order business called Perkins Products Co. to sell his concoctions through magazine advertisements. In 1920, Perkins moved his company to Hastings, Nebraska.

One of Perkins's more popular products was a concentrated drink mix called Fruit-Smack, available in six flavors at an economical price. Unfortunately, shipping the four-ounce glass bottles of syrup was costly and the bottles frequently leaked or broke in the mail. In 1927, Perkins devised a

method to dehydrate Fruit-Smack so the resulting powder could be packaged in paper envelopes. He then designed and printed envelopes with the product's new name: Kool-Ade (which he later changed to Kool-Aid).

Perkins initially offered Kool-Aid by direct mail and priced Kool-Aid to retail for ten cents a packet. In 1929, he distributed Kool-Aid (available in strawberry, cherry, lemon-lime, grape, orange, and raspberry) through food brokers to grocery stores nationwide.

By 1931, the strong demand for Kool-Aid prompted Perkins to stop making his other products and devote all his attention to Kool-Aid. He reduced the price of Kool-Aid to five cents a packet in 1933 and moved the entire Kool-Aid operation to Chicago. By 1950, Perkins employed approximately 350 workers.

NEANDERTHAL MAN

n August 1856, German quarry workers excavating the limestone rock from a cave in the Neander Valley, near the city of Düsseldorf, discovered an assortment of bones, a skull, and a variety of stone tools embedded in the cave floor. The quarry workers brought their finds to a local schoolmaster, Johann Karl Fuhlrott, who noted the similarities between the skeletal remains and

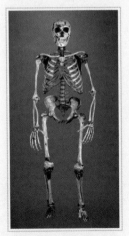

an illustration of a gorilla's skeleton. Fuhlrott also noticed that, unlike modern humans, the skull had a sloping forehead and a prominent eyebrow ridge. Suspecting the bones were an important archaeological discovery, Fuhlrott shared the bones with anatomist Hermann Schaaffhausen, and together, they announced the find in 1857 and suggested that the bones belonged to a savage race.

In 1864, paleontologist William King of Galway, Ireland, announced that the bones belonged to a new species related to human beings, which he dubbed *Homo neanderthalesis*. Similar skeletons discovered in 1886 in a cave in Spy, Belgium, substantiated the theory that Neanderthal man is an early human. DNA analysis has proven that Neanderthals are a separate species. Neanderthals lived for more than 300,000 years and died out 28,000 years ago.

TEA BAGS

I n 1908, New York tea merchant Thomas Sullivan decided to save money by sending his customers samples of tea in small silken bags that were hand-sewn shut rather than in pricier small metal tins. When orders began pouring in and Sullivan shipped tea orders, the customers complained that the tea had arrived in the standard loose form. They had expected to receive their new tea orders in the convenient tea bags he had sent for them to sample. Restaurant and coffee shop owners demonstrated for Sullivan how they brewed the tea leaves still enclosed in the permeable bag, enlightening the tea merchant who suddenly realized the potential of his inadvertent invention.

In response to criticism that the mesh on the silk was too fine, Sullivan developed sachets made of gauze and tied to a string—the first intentionally made tea bags—launching a virtual tea bag revolution.

In the 1920s, tea bags went into commercial production, and while the bags achieved widespread popularity in the United States, the British resisted such unorthodox tea-making methods. In 1930, William Hermanson, working for the Technical Paper Corp. in Boston, patented the heat-sealed paper tea bag. In 1953, Joseph Tetley & Co. introduced and popularized tea bags in Britain, and while tea bags accounted for less than 3 percent of the British market in the early 1960s, today tea bags comprise 96 percent of the British tea market.

DRY CLEANING

n 1855, a maid working in the home of Jean Baptiste Jolly, the owner of a dye-works in Paris, France, accidentally tipped over an unlit oil lamp, spilling some camphene (distilled turpentine) on a tablecloth. When the maid blotted up the mess, Jolly noticed that the stained area had

become brighter and cleaner than the rest of the tablecloth. Inspired, Jolly began offering a new service through his dye-works factory called *nettoyage à sec*

("dry cleaning"), so named because the new process did not require any soap or water.

Unfortunately, camphene was highly flammable and left the clothes suffused with an unpleasant odor. Attempts to substitute for camphene with naphtha, benzene, or gasoline proved equally impractical. In the 1930s, the dry-cleaning industry adopted perchloroethylene as the favored dry-cleaning solvent. Regrettably, laboratory studies show that breathing perchloroethylene (also called "perc") causes kidney and liver damage and cancer in animals, and the U.S. Environmental Protection Agency reports that repeated exposure to large amounts of perc in air may cause cancer in humans.

Today, the dry-cleaning industry is seeking a nontoxic replacement for perc.

TINKER TOYS

round 1910, Charles Pajeau, a stonemason from Evanston, Illinois, discovered that his children built structures by sticking pencils and sticks into empty spools of thread. Inspired by his children's ingenuity, Pajeau worked in his garage to create a shorter, wheel-like spool with a series of holes running around the circumference and several other basic wooden parts so his children could build a wide variety of three-dimensional structures.

Realizing he had created a marketable construction toy that let kids tinker for hours, Pajeau teamed up with Robert Petit to found the Toy Tinkers Company, and the two men displayed Tinker Toys, packaged in a cardboard canister with a metal lid and

bottom, at the 1914 American Toy Fair. Unfortunately, Tinker Toys went unnoticed.

Undaunted, Pajeau and Petit built an elaborate Tinker Toy display in the pharmacy of Grand Central Station in New York City so passersby would see how children could play with the creations they built with Tinker Toy parts. Within days, the display generated thousands of sales.

At Christmastime, Pajeau and Petit hired several midgets to dress in elf costumes and play with Tinker Toys in a display window of a Chicago department store as a publicity stunt. Within a year, more than one million Tinker Toy sets had been sold.

CHEMOTHERAPY

During World War II, General Dwight D. Eisenhower secretly stockpiled one hundred tons of mustard gas aboard the SS *John Harvey*, a ship stationed in Italy's Bari Harbor. In December 1943, German air strikes destroyed the *John Harvey*, and during the following days and weeks, survivors began to develop signs of mustard gas

exposure. Autopsies of the victims reported abnormally low white blood cell counts and suppression of myeloid cell lines.

Doctors deduced that if mustard gas destroyed white blood cells, it might similarly destroy cancer. In clinical trials, Dr. Louis Goodman and Dr. Alfred Gilman of Yale University injected nitrogen mustards into patients with advanced lymphomas (cancers of particular white blood cells) and certain types of leukemia (in which neoplastic bone marrow overproduces white blood cells). Although none of these nitrogen mustards cured any type of human cancer, they profoundly reduced the tumors, raising the hope that science might ultimately find curative chemical substances and launching the field of chemotherapy.

CALIFORNIA GOLD RUSH

I n the fall of 1847, carpenter James W. Marshall began building a sawmill to produce lumber in partnership with Captain John Sutter on the captain's 48,000 acres of land in Coloma, California. Marshall's crew dug a ditch to carry water from the South Fork of the American River for power. Having dug the tailrace (the lower end of the ditch) far too shallow, the crew spent several weeks deepening the tailrace to let the water flow unobstructed through the mill. The flowing water carried away sand and

dirt but left a heavier metal to accumulate in the deepening ditch.

On the morning of January 24, 1848, Marshall noticed several flakes of metal in the

tailrace water, which he recognized as gold. "I went down as usual," recalled Marshall in *Hutchings' California Magazine* in 1857, "and after shutting off the water from the race I stepped into it, near the lower end, and there, upon the rock, about six inches beneath the surface of the water, I discovered the gold."

Marshall tested the metal with a lye bath (because sodium hydroxide dissolves most metals, but not gold). Four days later, he rode to Sutter's fort and showed the gold to the captain, who performed several tests on the metal, confirming the find was indeed gold. The next day, Sutter went to the mill site and asked all the workers to keep the discovery a secret (to prevent his laborers at the fort from deserting him). However, word spread quickly, triggering the California Gold Rush of 1849, and Sutter's workers abandoned him to search for gold.

KEVLAR

n 1965, Stephanie Kwolek, one of the few women chemists at the DuPont Pioneering Research Laboratory in Wilmington, Delaware, dissolved a polymer in a test tube in an attempt to develop lightweight, heat-resistant fibers to reinforce radial tires. "Ordinarily a polymer solution sort of reminds you of molasses, although it may not be as thick," explained Kwolek. "And it's generally transparent. This polymer solution poured almost like water, and it was cloudy. I thought, 'There's something different about this. This may be very useful.'"

Normally, the researchers would discard a cloudy, iridescent fluid, but Kwolek, convinced that this unusual solution could be spun into fibers, spent several days persuading technician Charles Smullen, who ran the "spinneret," to extrude her solution into a fiber and test its physical properties. (Smullen feared that the cloudy solution would gunk up the machine.) The test results revealed a remarkably strong, stiff, and yet lightweight fiber—five times stronger than steel, but about half the density of fiberglass.

DuPont instructed its Pioneering Research Laboratory to seek a viable commercial version of Kwolek's new super-strength fiber, and six years later, in 1971, the company began marketing the material as Kevlar, best known as the bulletproof fabric from which bulletproof vests and body armor are made (saving thousands of lives). Kevlar is also used to make fiber-optic cables, military helmets, skis, bicycle tires, yacht sails, ropes, and brake pads.

HALL & OATES

n 1967, Daryl Hall, a senior at Temple University, sang lead with his band, the Temptones, to compete in a battle-of-the-bands in the Adelphi Ballroom in Philadelphia, Pennsylvania. Another Temple University student, freshman John Oates, competed in the contest, leading his soul

band, the Masters. A gang fight broke out, and both Hall and Oates fled from the scene in the same freight elevator. Admiring each other's talents and recognizing their shared musical interests, Hall and Oates decided to team up to sing and perform together in various rhythm-and-blues and doo-wop groups.

When Oates transferred to another college, Hall formed the soft-rock band Gulliver. After earning a degree in journalism, Oates rekindled his friendship with Hall, who invited him to join Gulliver. Shortly afterward, Gulliver broke up. Oates traveled through Europe. Hall continued pursuing a music career, singing backup for the Stylistics, the Delfonics, and the Intruders. When Oates returned from his travels, he reunited with Hall, and the twosome began to perform around Philadelphia as Hall and Oates, writing their own acoustic songs together.

In 1973, Hall and Oates released their album *Abandoned Luncheonette*, yielding the Top Ten hit "She's Gone," which became a number one hit on the R&B charts when it was covered by the band Tavares. The duo is best known for their hit singles "Rich Girl," "Kiss on My List," "Private Eyes," "I Can't Go For That (No Can Do)," "Maneater," "Out of Touch," and "Sara Smile."

DNA STRUCTURE

n 1946, during his third year studying ornithology at the University of Chicago, 18-year-old James Watson read *What Is Life?*—a book that changed his life. In the book, quantum physicist Erwin Schrödinger asserts that the genetic code transferred from parent to child could only exist at the molecular level since those instructions had to fit inside a single cell. After graduation, Watson proceeded to Indiana University to study viruses in the hopes of finding the code in the simplest life form on earth.

In 1951, after receiving his doctorate at age twenty-two, Watson attended a conference in Naples, Italy, sat in on a lecture by biophysicist Maurice Wilkins of King's College, London, and saw a molecule of deoxyribonucleic acid (better known as DNA) rendered by X-ray crystallography. Realizing that DNA might hold the key to genetic information,

Watson obtained a fellowship at the Cavendish Laboratory at the University of Cambridge (where X-ray crystallography had been developed), determined to unleash the secret of DNA.

At the Cavendish Laboratory, Watson met Francis Crick, a physicist who had helped develop radar during World War II. Crick, similarly influenced by Schrödinger's *What Is Life?*, had crossed over to molecular biology and was conducting research to earn his doctorate in protein structure. Watson and Crick recognized each other as kindred spirits and joined forces to understand the structure of DNA.

Based on research by Maurice Wilkins and the X-ray pictures of DNA crystals by chemist Rosalind Franklin, Watson and Crick used big 3-D molecular models to build a model of the molecular structure of DNA. On February 28, 1953, Watson and Crick figured out that the structure of DNA is a double helix that looks like a twisted ladder and "upzips" to reproduce itself, carrying hereditary information via the sequence of certain chemicals on the successive rungs of the ladder. The two scientists adjourned to the Eagle pub in Cambridge to toast their discovery, and Crick proclaimed to his fellow patrons that he and Watson had just unearthed "the secret of life."

SCOTCHGARD

n 1952, 3M researchers Patsy Sherman and Sam Smith, trying to create a synthetic rubber material for jet aircraft fuel hoses, mixed up a latex solution. One day, a laboratory technician accidentally spilled a sample of the substance on her tennis shoe. The technician could not wash the stuff off with soapy water or any organic solvents, and the stained spot on her tennis shoe also resisted soiling.

"No one had ever thought of a fabric that could repel both oil and water," recalled Sherman in *Women Invent!: Two Centuries of Discoveries That Have Shaped Our World*. "So someone got the idea to dip a little piece of fabric in the latex and dry it out. Then we held the fabric under water. Sure enough, water just bounced right off it. When we dropped oil on it, it beaded up. Nothing would wet this piece of fabric. We thought maybe there was a better use for this material than for making jet aircraft hoses."

Sherman and Smith realized this substance might be used to make textiles resist water and oil stains and went to work to enhance the compound's ability to repel liquids. Scotchgard became one of 3M's most profitable products and launched the company into the fabric protection business, a direction 3M had never planned to explore.

MAUVE

n 1856, eighteen-year-old William Perkin, at home with his family during his Easter vacation from the Royal College of Chemistry in London, attempted to synthesize quinine, the only effective drug against malaria, from toluidine, a derivative of coal tar. He oxidized ally-o-toluidine with potassium dichromate, creating a reddish-brown sludge. Undaunted, he started over, using aniline, which, unbeknownst to Perkin, contained a small amount of toluidine. The result was a useless black solid.

When Perkin tried to wash the substance from the flask with alcohol, he noticed that the alcohol turned a vivid purple color. Intrigued, Perkin poured the purple solution on a cloth and discovered that it dyed the fabric. He extracted the purple dye from the black mass and sent a sample to a well-known British dye works to test on silk and cotton. The test confirmed that Perkin had indeed produced the world's first synthetic dye.

Perkin patented his discovery, persuaded his wealthy father and brother to finance the construction of a factory, and devised a procedure to produce the dye on an industrial level. His affordable purple dye became widely known by its French name *mauve*, and its great success gave birth to the synthetic dye industry.

FOLSOM SITE

n September 1908, African-American cowboy and former slave George McJunkin, a ranch hand at the Crowfoot Ranch, near the town of Folsom, New Mexico, rode his horse along the banks of the Wild Horse Arroyo to inspect the fence lines for any damage caused by a recent flash flood. The storm had washed away sections of the gully, and McJunkin noticed several large bones protruding from the side of the Wild Horse Arroyo. He pulled out a large bone, which he did not recognize as any cattle or bison bones he had ever seen before. Deducing that the bones belonged to an extinct species

of bison, he attempted to bring the discovery to the attention of archaeologists—without success.

In 1926, four years after McJunkin's death, Jesse Figgins, director of the Colorado Museum of Natural History, investigated the Folsom site and concluded that the bones belonged to a species of bison that had gone extinct at the end of the Ice Age. A flint spearhead found lying between the ribs of a bison revealed that people had lived in the Americas more than 7,000 years before the previously determined date of 1,000 B.C.E.

LIQUORICE ALLSORTS

n the late 1890s, British confectionery Bassett's created several different types and flavors of licorice candies—Buttons, Chips, Cubes, Nuggets, Plugs, Rocks, and Twists. In 1899, while trying to sell his sweets to a wholesaler in Leicester, Bassett's salesman Charlie Thompson met with constant rejection—until he accidentally dropped his

case of samples, creating a colorful assortment of licorice treats on the floor. The store owner, entranced by the colorful mixture of candies, immediately ordered a batch, inspiring Thompson to name his accidental combination of confections

"Liquorice Allsorts." Realizing that Thompson had literally stumbled onto something, the company began to mass-produce the allsorts, which became very popular.

VENUS DE MILO

n February 1820, Greek farmer Yorgos Bottonis and his son, Antonio, were clearing away stones in a field near the ruins of an ancient theater, a short distance from Castro, the capital of the Aegean island of Melos. They accidentally uncovered the entrance to an underground cave. Inside the cave, they found a fine marble statue in two pieces with several other marble fragments.

Bottonis reported his find to the village priest, Reverend Oiconomos, who invited French consul Louis Brest to see the armless statue of the Roman goddess Venus and buy it for France for 20,000 francs. Hesitant to disperse such a large sum of government money, Brest wrote to the French ambassador in Constantinople and awaited a response.

In April, a French ship happened to dock at Melos and French naval officer Jules Dumont d'Urville went to see the statue. Bottonis offered to sell it for 1,200 francs, and d'Urville sailed to Constantinople to relay this offer to the French ambassador. The ambassador sent Count Marcellus, a member of his embassy, to Melos to procure the statue. However, when Marcellus arrived in Melos, he discovered that Bottonis, having grown tired of waiting for payment, had sold the statue for 4,800 francs to Turkish prince Nikolai Morusi in Constantinople, and the statue was being loaded aboard a ship bound for that city.

The three Frenchmen—Brest, d'Urville, and Marcellus—protested and offered Bottonis 6,000 francs for the statue. Having not yet been paid by Morusi, Bottonis agreed. The statue was taken off the ship, loaded instead on a ship to France on May 25, and presented to King Louis XVIII in October. In 1821, the Venus de Milo was delivered to the Louvre museum in Paris, where it stands on public display to this day.

PULSARS

A t the University of Cambridge in July 1967, graduate student Jocelyn Bell, pursuing her doctorate degree in astronomy, noticed a strange burst of radiation while analyzing the data generated by a radio telescope designed by her advisor, Antony Hewish. Bell and Hewish had been using the radio telescope to study the scintillation of radio waves generated by quasars as they passed through the interplanetary medium. The signal Bell detected did not scintillate like a quasar, star, or any known man-made interference. Instead, a particular patch of sky emitted a regular, pulsating series of signals spaced 1.3 seconds apart. At first, Bell and Hewish thought they had detected a signal from an extraterrestrial civilization, and they jokingly nicknamed the source LGM-1 for "Little Green Men."

When Bell detected a similar series of pulses arriving 1.2 seconds apart from a completely different patch of sky, the two astronomers ruled out extraterrestrial life as a possible source of the signal—since the odds of two different groups of extraterrestrials on different sides of the universe attempting to send signals toward earth simultaneously were infinitesimal. Over the Christmas holiday, Bell discovered two more sources of pulsating signals.

In February 1968, Hewish publicly announced the discovery of the first pulsar—without knowing the nature of the source. Soon afterward, Austrian-born astrophysicist Thomas Gold, an astronomy professor at Cornell University, showed that pulsars are actually neutron stars—extremely dense stars formed from collapsed remnants of a supernova—that emit radio waves as they spin, which we on earth see as a series of pulses, like a beam of light from a lighthouse.

ICE-CREAM SODA

Robert M. Green of Philadelphia operated a soda fountain at the 1874 semi-centennial exhibition of the Franklin Institute, held near city hall. At the time, soda fountains sold a mixture of soda water, fruit syrup, shaved ice, and sweet cream called an "ice-cream soda," despite the fact that the concoction did not contain ice cream. While serving these sweet-cream sodas, Green ran out of cream. He bought two small pitchers from a neighboring crockery concessionaire and raced to Henry Snyder's confectionery to buy vanilla ice cream.

Green planned to let the ice cream melt before substituting it for the cream. But when he encountered a line of eager customers upon his return, he decided to simply spoon the ice cream into the sodas, creating the world's first genuine ice-cream soda. The invention was a big hit, and by the time the exhibition closed, Green was making $400 a day.

Despite the popularity of ice-cream sodas, blue laws in several states prohibited the sale of ice-cream sodas on Sundays because the beverage contained carbonated soda water. To get around those laws, soda-fountain operators served the ice cream with the flavored syrup but no soda and called the resultant dish a sundae, spelled *sundae* to avoid any religious backlash from the devout.

LITHIUM

While incarcerated by the Japanese as a prisoner of war at Changi Prison in Singapore during World War II, Australian doctor John F. Cade observed some of his fellow inmates exhibiting erratic behavior. He suspected that his captors had given a toxin to these inmates that affected their brains until they urinated, which then removed the toxin from their bodies.

After the war, Cade, working as a medical superintendent and psychiatrist at Bundoora Repatriation Mental Hospital in Melbourne, experimentally injected urine from mentally ill patients into guinea pigs. Noting that the urine of schizophrenics and depressives killed guinea pigs, Cade hypothesized that the urine of the mentally ill patients contained excess uric acid. To make the uric acid more water soluble, Cade added lithium carbonate to the urine and injected the solution into more guinea pigs. This time, the urine did not kill the guinea pigs but instead made the rodents lethargic.

After taking lithium carbonate himself to make sure the compound produced no ill effect, Cade tested lithium carbonate on patients diagnosed with chronic mania and manic-depressive syndrome. He observed that the lithium treatment quelled mania. Cade deduced that a lithium deficiency caused mania, and lithium quickly became a widely used drug to treat chronic mania and bipolar disorders.

BAN CHIANG ARTIFACTS

n the summer of 1966, while going door to door canvassing political opinion in the village of Ban Chiang in northeast Thailand for his senior thesis, Harvard University student Stephen Young tripped over the root of a kapok tree and landed face-to-face with the rims of some ceramic pots protruding from the earth. Recent monsoons had exposed the unglazed earthenware. Young decided

to bring some samples back to government officials in Bangkok.

Young had stumbled upon the earliest known Bronze Age site in Southeast Asia, dating back to as early as 2000 B.C.E. Unfortunately, local villagers looted artifacts from the immediate area extensively. Still, when Chester Gorman, an archaeologist from the University of Pennsylvania, arrived in 1974 and dug beneath the middle of a nearby village street, he excavated eighteen tons of artifacts for study.

Ban Chiang is one of only five UNESCO World Heritage Sites in Thailand, and the village's preserved excavation site contains unearthed pottery and skeletal remains.

BUBBLE WRAP

n 1957, American inventor Alfred Fielding and his partner, Swiss inventor Marc Chavannes, working in Hawthorne, New Jersey, attempted to develop a machine to produce plastic wallpaper with a paper backing. Instead, their machine produced sheets of plastic filled with air bubbles.

"It took us a while to figure out what to do with that," recalled Fielding, "until we figured packaging was the way to go." Fielding and Chavannes named their accidental

invention AirCap material, and after raising $9,000 to develop the product further, built a crude, six-inch-wide pilot machine that could make AirCap material continuously. They formed Sealed Air Corporation, raised $85,000 in stock offerings, and began full-scale production of bubble wrap in 1960.

Unfortunately, the AirCap bubbles leaked, slowly deflating. By 1965, Fielding and Chavannes developed a machine that would apply a special coating on the outside of the bubble to prevent air loss. Later, the company added a barrier coating on the inside of the bubbles.

In 1971, Fielding and Chavannes recruited T. J. Dermot Dunphy, a graduate of Oxford University and Harvard Business School, to head the Sealed Air Corporation. Under Dunphy's direction, annual sales went from $5 million to $500 million by 1994. Today, Sealed Air sells dozens of packaging materials, including Jiffy padded envelopes, polyethylene foams, and Instapak, a system that pours a polyurethane liquid that expands into foam cushioning.

LITHOGRAPHY

n 1795, Alois Senefelder, a 24-year-old author determined to print his own work in Munich, Germany, discovered that a mixture of soap, wax, and lampblack (black pigment collected from soot) formed an excellent material for writing on copperplates. When the solution dried, it became firm and acid resistant. To practice writing backward, Senefelder obtained some inexpensive pieces of Kellheim limestone and polished the surfaces.

One day when his mother asked him to jot down a laundry list, Senefelder used a grease pencil to write the list on one of the polished stones. Before erasing the list, he decided to use acid to etch away the surface of the stone to see if the words written in grease pencil would remain in relief. Miraculously, they did—even though the markings were too shallow to retain ink.

Senefelder had accidentally stumbled upon a way to make stone take ink chemically rather than mechanically. He called the process *lithography* (Greek for "stone printing"), perfected the chemical procedure, and developed a series of lithographic presses, turning lithography into the dominant method for printing pictures in books. As for his desire to be an author, Senefelder wrote a textbook on lithography in 1818.

BATTERIES

I n 1786, Italian physiologist Luigi Galvani, a professor at the University of Bologna, noticed that the legs of dead frogs twitched when they were hung from brass hooks on an iron railing. Galvani erroneously concluded that the dead frogs contained "animal electricity," a theory he published in his book *Commentary on the Effect of Electricity on Muscular Motion*.

When fellow professor Allesandro Volta, a physicist at the University of Pavia, read Galvani's book, he reached a different conclusion. Volta deduced that the frogs' legs were completing an electrical circuit between the brass hooks (composed primarily of copper) and the

iron railing. Volta explained that the frog tissue allowed currents to flow between two dissimilar metals.

To prove his theory, Volta produced the first practical battery by making "cells" from two different metals, such as silver and zinc, separated by a disk of cardboard moistened with an acidic solution. Volta then connected these cells in series to make a battery—an array of single *galvanic* cells (named for Galvani), which produced *voltage* (named for Volta).

DIPPIN' DOTS

n 1987, while making homemade ice cream with a neighbor, microbiologist Curt Jones wished that he could freeze ice cream faster to eliminate the icy taste. "Wait a minute," said Jones, "I know how to do this." At his job at Alltech, an animal health company in Lexington, Kentucky, Jones had been experimenting with various quick-freezing-techniques to preserve yogurt bacteria cultures for use in animal feeds. He brought a pint of homemade ice-cream mix from an old family recipe to work and used liquid nitrogen vapor to flash-freeze it. The result? The first tiny pellets of ice cream—yielding a richer, fresher taste because they contained almost no ice crystals or air.

Jones patented his process, quit his job, and opened his first store in a shop-

ping mall in Lexington, half-heartedly dubbing his invention Yoglet. Finally, while driving home to Southern Illinois with his wife and daughter for Christmas, Jones said, "You know, we oughta call a bunch of our friends and make some ice cream for 'em and then let them just come up with names." At that get-together, a guest named Vonda Jones (no relation to Curt) suggested "Dip-in-Dots," which Curt mistakenly heard as "Dippin' Dots." "That's perfect!" he exclaimed, not realizing he had stumbled upon the name himself.

Based on his childhood love for Neapolitan ice cream (a container of one-third vanilla, one-third chocolate, and one-third strawberry ice cream), Jones mixed together frozen beads of vanilla, chocolate, and strawberry. While serving Dippin' Dots at a kiosk at the now defunct Opryland USA theme park, Jones ran out of strawberry beads for his Neapolitan mix, so he mixed in banana beads instead. "And that's how we came up with Banana Split, which became our number one seller for many years."

JOHNSTON ATOLL

O n September 2, 1796, the American brig *Sally*, commanded by Captain Joseph Pierpoint, accidentally ran aground on a shoal in the central Pacific Ocean, between the Hawaiian Islands and the Marshall Islands. Pierpoint had inadvertently discovered a sunken island made from layers of basaltic lava upon which corals around its fringes had continued to grow, creating a

broad, shallow platform of about fifty square miles with two small islands.

In 1807, the crew of the frigate HMS *Cornwallis* rediscovered the atoll. The ship's captain, Charles J. Johnston, named the larger of the two islands after himself.

In 1926, President Calvin Coolidge designated the Johnston Atoll as a federal bird refuge. In 1934, President Franklin D. Roosevelt placed the atoll under U.S. Navy control, and beginning in the late 1940s, the United States military carried out nuclear testing at Johnston Atoll. In 1971, the government began stockpiling chemical weapons on Johnston Island. By 2005, the military had intentionally incinerated the chemicals and abandoned the atoll.

On January 6, 2009, President George W. Bush established the Pacific Remote Islands Marine National Monument, which includes Johnston Atoll National Wildlife Refuge.

VELCRO

While hiking with his dog in the Swiss Alps in 1948, electrical engineer George de Mestral passed through a patch of brush, which quickly covered his jacket and his dog's fur with cockleburs. When he returned home, de Mestral removed one of the cockleburs from his trousers and, wondering how something so small could attach itself so tenaciously to his clothing and his dog's mane, examined it under his microscope. He discovered that the cocklebur was covered with hooks that clung to the small loops of fabric in his clothing and the strands of hair in animal fur. In this way, nature assured that seeds inside the burr would be dispersed over great dis-

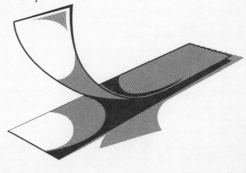

tances by animals or birds, increasing the cocklebur plant's odds of proliferation.

Intrigued by nature's design, de Mestral attempted to create a fastening system using two strips of fabric, one embedded with lots of small hooks and the other sewn with an overabundance of tiny loops. He worked with a weaver in France to design tough hooks and soft loops made from nylon to achieve the desired effect, perfecting the design in 1955. De Mestral called his ingenious fastening tape Velcro, a combination of the words *velour* and *crochet* (French for "velvet" and "hooks"). Through Velcro Industries, he was soon selling more than 180 million feet of Velcro every year, used to secure clothing, shoes, sports equipment, luggage, wallets, toys, home furnishings, medical supplies, and military equipment. Even NASA found a use for it—fastening objects in place aboard space shuttle missions.

PIGGY BANKS

uring the Middle Ages, banking institutions did not exist in England, and people commonly stored their money at home in kitchen jars, typically made from an orange-colored clay called *pygg*—which, during the time of the Saxons, would have been pronounced "pug." As the pronunciation of the letter *y* changed from "u" to "i," the word *pygg* eventually came to be pronounced "pig." Meanwhile, the Old English word for pig (*picga*) evolved into the Middle English word *pigge*, possibly because the animals rolled around in pygg mud.

As the English language evolved over the next two hundred years, the words *pygg* and *pigge* came to be pronounced similarly, and the British soon forgot that pygg once referred to the clay pots, jars, and plates. People saved their money in pygg jars, which became known in eighteenth century England as pig jars or pig banks, prompting potters to fashion the jars into the shape of pigs—which delighted both adults and children.

BIG BANG

n 1964, Arno Penzias and Robert Wilson, two scientists at Bell Laboratories in Holmdel, New Jersey, modified a radio antenna to study radio signals bouncing off echo balloon satellites. Yet wherever they pointed the antenna in the sky,

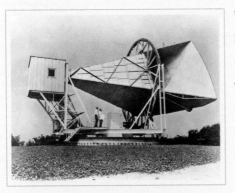

they heard static. They figured something was causing interference with the antenna. After capturing two pigeons that were nesting in the horn-shaped antenna and cleaning off the

pigeon droppings, the two scientists still detected the staticky signal wherever they pointed the antenna.

Convinced that the noise was coming from outside the galaxy, Penzias and Wilson exchanged their findings with astronomers at Princeton University. Together, they realized that the staticky signal was the residual microwave radiation leftover from the Big Bang, the massive explosion of highly condensed matter that astronomers theorized had occurred fifteen billion years ago at the start of the universe.

In 1978, Penzias and Wilson were awarded the Noble Prize in physics for their discovery.

NYLON

I n 1930, chemist Dr. Julian W. Hill worked with a team of researchers at the DuPont Company in Wilmington, Delaware, trying to create larger polymers by adjusting the amount of water in a batch of carbon- and alcohol-based molecules. The team devised a concoction that DuPont's

research head, Wallace H. Carothers, dismissed as useless.

Undaunted, Hill stuck a heated glass rod into a beaker containing the polymer and discovered that the substance pulled like taffy and became silky when stretched at room temperature. One day, while Carothers was out of the office, Hill and his colleagues tried to see how far they could stretch the strands of polymer down the corridor, pulling them out into a remarkably long and durable string. Recognizing the silky appearance of the extended strands, Hill realized that he and his colleagues, through their horseplay, had accidentally used "cold drawing" to orient the polymer molecules and increase the strength of the compound, creating a viable substitute for silk.

DuPont introduced the synthetic silk substance as "nylon" at the 1939 World's Fair in New York. Nylon stockings cost twice the price of silk stockings, but women gladly paid the price because nylon was stronger and more sheer than silk. During World War II, the United States government restricted the use of nylon to the military to make parachutes, rope, tents, and aircraft tires. Nylon has also been used to make luggage and hair and toothbrush bristles. DuPont never trademarked the word *nylon*, determined that the nylon would become the generic name for polyamide fiber.

"STILL LIFE WITH FLOWERS"

n July 1990, John Kuhn, a commercial real estate agent working part-time as an art prospector for a Chicago auction house, was examining antique furniture in the home of a retired, middle-class couple living in Milwaukee, Wisconsin. He spotted a still-life painting on the wall that

looked like the work of Vincent van Gogh, the legendary nineteenth century Dutch post-impressionist painter. "When I told them what I thought it was, they laughed," Kuhn told the *Chicago Tribune* in 1991. "They didn't believe it."

The couple had inherited the painting from a relative named Gebhard Adolf Guyer, a onetime Swiss banker who collected art and immigrated to the United States after the start of World War II. Guyer sold much of his art collection to the Wildenstein Gallery in New York and willed a few paintings to relatives before his death in the late 1950s. The painting had been hanging in the Milwaukee home for more than thirty years.

With permission from the couple, Kuhn placed the painting in the backseat of his Volkswagen Jetta and drove to Chicago to have the artwork appraised by experts. In November, Leslie Hindman Auctioneers shipped the painting to Han van Crimpen, senior research curator at the Rijksmuseum in Amsterdam and one of the world's leading van Gogh authorities. Van Crimpen and other researchers declared the oil painting, dubbed "Still Life With Flowers" and signed only with a "V" in the lower left corner, as an authentic van Gogh. Leslie Hindman Auctioneers eventually sold the painting for $1.43 million to an anonymous private collector.

BRANDY

I n the sixteenth century, Dutch merchants decided to ship wine from the Charente region of France to the Netherlands, despite the fact that Charente wine was substandard compared with wines from the Bordeaux region sixty miles south. The Dutch merchants also decided to lessen the high cost of shipping the wine to the Netherlands by distilling out the water  from the wine, reducing the weight and the shipping costs. As an added benefit, distilling the wine would preserve the freshness of the wine on the voyage.

Upon arriving at their destination, the Dutch merchants intended to dilute the wine syrup with water, bringing it back to its original viscosity and lower alcohol content. However, after tasting the condensed wine and finding it far more palatable—and potent—than the original acidic Charente wine, the Dutch decided to market the new product as *brandewign* (Dutch for "burnt wine"). The English, regular importers of Dutch goods, anglicized the name to "brandy wine," which they ultimately shortened to "brandy." Brandy is also called Cognac, after the French town in the Charente region where the burnt wine originated.

ROGAINE

n 1980, Dr. Anthony R. Zappacosta, a kidney specialist in Bryn Mawr, Pennsylvania, noticed that a 38-year-old dialysis patient, who had been nearly bald since age twenty, suddenly grew ample hair on his scalp after taking minoxidil pills for high blood pressure. The unexpected side effect surprised Zappacosta even more because his patient was receiving shots of a hormone that frequently caused hair loss. Zappacosta wrote a letter to the *New England Journal of Medicine*, revealing minoxidil's effect on hair growth.

Dermatologist Virginia Fiedler-Weiss of the University of Illinois Medical Center in Chicago reasoned that the drug would promote hair growth—without lowering blood pressure and causing undesirable side effects—if it was applied topically. She prepared a lotion from crushed minoxidil tablets and instructed three of her patients (made bald by severe allergies to their own hair follicles) to apply a thin layer to their scalps twice a day. Within weeks, two of the patients were growing normal hair.

Meanwhile, Zappacosta's letter to the *New England Journal of Medicine* had prompted Upjohn, the maker of minoxidil, to concoct a minoxidil lotion for the scalp and market it as Rogaine. Unfortunately, minoxidil seems to grow hair only if a person uses it indefinitely.

CRO-MAGNON MAN

n March 1868, French workmen clearing away the sloping side of a limestone cliff to widen the railroad tracks for a new station in the village of Les Eyzies unearthed a small, completely buried cave near a rock called Cro-Magnon (French for "great cavity"). Inside

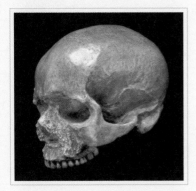

the cave, the workmen found flint tools, animal bones, and human skulls.

The managers brought construction to an abrupt halt, and soon afterward, geologist Louis Lartet excavated the shelter and found five human skeletons, including an infant, that had been buried with shell beads and ivory pendants. These tall, slender prototypical *Homo sapiens* lived 40,000 years ago during the Ice Age, rivaled and became the successors to the more robust Neanderthals, and eventually spawned modern-day Europeans.

The tools and artifacts of Cro-Magnon people can be viewed in the Musée National de Préhistoire in Dordogne, France. The skeletons of these Cro-Magnon people are kept at the Musée de l'Homme in Paris.

WORLD WIDE WEB

n 1989, British computer scientist Tim Berners-Lee proposed to build a tool by which researchers at CERN, the European particle physics laboratory in Geneva, Switzerland, could exchange ideas and publish papers via the Internet. When he received no reply from CERN, Berners-Lee began developing his World Wide Web— a network of centrally stored, hypertext documents that could be viewed by browser programs installed on individual computers.

Berners-Lee wrote the Hypertext Transfer Protocol (the language computers would use to communicate hypertext documents via the Internet—the "http" at the beginning of web page addresses), devised a method to locate the documents (assigning each document its own unique address—now called a URL), and created the first browser (a program for retrieving and viewing documents). Berners-Lee also wrote the software for the first web server (the computer that stores and transmits web pages) and created HTML (the Hypertext Markup Language that describes the format and layout of material on the page).

In 1991, having yet to receive any response from CERN, Berners-Lee set up the first web server and made his World Wide Web browser and web server software available on the Internet for free, posting its availability in various newsgroups. The first web page address was http://info.cern.ch/hypertext/WWW/TheProject.html.

When World Wide Web users began setting up their own web servers, Berners-Lee linked his server to theirs. As the number of users increased, the mass appeal skyrocketed. Determined to keep the Web universally accessible, Berners-Lee never patented his invention or charged royalties—creating the information superhighway, which CERN ultimately embraced.

WHEATIES

I n 1921, a Minneapolis health clinician (whose name has been lost to history) mixed a batch of bran gruel for his patients and accidentally spilled some of the mix on the hot stove. The gruel crackled, sizzled, and turned into crisp flakes.

The clinician tasted the grilled gruel flakes and realized they had potential as a breakfast cereal. He brought a sample of the flakes to the Washburn Crosby Company, where executives, fancying the idea, invited the clinician to use a laboratory to turn his gruel flakes into a marketable product. Despite the clinician's best efforts, the flakes were too fragile, crumbling to dust when packaged for sale.

Washburn Crosby's head miller, Scottish immigrant George Cormack, took over the project, attempting to toughen the flakes to prevent them from being pulverized inside a cereal box. Cormack tested thirty-six varieties of wheat before hitting upon a durable flake in 1924. That same year, the company marketed the cereal as Washburn's Gold Medal Whole Wheat Flakes—in the hopes of capitalizing on the success of its Gold Medal Flour. Lackluster sales prompted the company to launch a companywide contest to find a catchier name. Jane Bausman, the wife of the export manager, proposed the name Wheaties, defeating runners-up Nutties and Gold Medal Wheat Flakes. In 1928, Washburn Crosby became General Mills, and in 1933, the company began advertising Wheaties with the slogan "The Breakfast of Champions."

PRUSSIAN BLUE

I n 1704, Heinrich Diesbach, a paint maker in Berlin, then the capital of Prussia, was making cochineal red dye-based pigment, which required iron sulfate and potash in addition to the red pigment from cochineal insects. While working in the laboratory of alchemist Johann Konrad Dippel, he accidentally used a batch of potash that had been contaminated with animal oil. The contaminated potash caused the red paint to turn extremely pale. Diesbach attempted to concentrate the red paint, which turned purple and then deep blue.

Unbeknownst to Diesbach, the oil reacted with the potash to form the purple-colored potassium ferrocyanide, which then combined with the iron sulfate to form the deep blue compound ferric ferrocyanide.

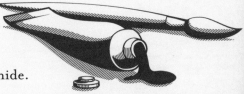

First used extensively to dye the uniforms of the Prussian army, the color became known as Prussian blue. Prized for its intense blue color, Prussian blue has been used by artists in paintings for centuries.

CHEESEBURGER

n 1923, sixteen-year-old Lionel Clark Sternberger, working as a cook at his father's steak restaurant, The Rite Spot, on Colorado Boulevard (then part of Route 66) in Pasadena, California, accidentally burned a hamburger—according to legend. Rather than throw the scorched patty away, Sternberger hid the charred spot under a slice of cheese. Having successfully concealed his blunder, Sternberger served the world's first cheeseburger to a customer, who was delighted by the new taste sensation.

Was the cheeseburger truly invented in Pasadena?

 The Pasadena Museum of History preserves an undated menu from The Rite Spot that lists the "Aristocratic Burger: the Original Hamburger with

Cheese," for 15 cents. That menu was produced in nearby Glendale by the Trapp Printing Co., which closed in 1939.

In a letter to the *Metropolitan News-Enterprise* in 2004, Gordon Gulack of El Monte offered eyewitness testimony. "When I was going to Pasadena High in the '20s, we used to go to a very small hamburger place run by Lionel Sternberger," wrote Gulack. "I can remember getting a cheeseburger."

LIQUID PAPER

n 1951, 27-year-old Bette Nesmith, working as an executive secretary at Texas Bank & Trust in San Antonio, Texas, ran into a problem with her new IBM electric typewriter. When she tried to fix her mistakes with a pencil eraser, the ink from the carbon-film ribbon in the new machine smudged the paper, creating a bigger mess.

Inspired by the holiday window painters who brushed over smudges and flaws in their work, Nesmith decided to paint over her mistakes with a bottle of white tempera paint and a watercolor brush. Nesmith's simple yet ingenious idea caught on with other secretaries at work, and by 1956, Nesmith was mixing

up batches of "Mistake Out," combining paint and other chemicals in her kitchen blender, and bottling the product in her garage.

When demand skyrocketed, she renamed the product "Liquid Paper" and applied for a patent and a trademark. By 1975, her company was making 25 million bottles of Liquid Paper a year, distributed to thirty-one countries. In 1979, Bette Nesmith sold her company to Gillette for $47.5 million.

BUCKYBALLS

n 1985, British chemist Harry Kroto worked with a group of chemists at Rice University in Houston, Texas, studying the large carbon molecules that astronauts had found drifting in space. The scientists hypothesized that these carbon molecules originated in old stars through nuclear fusion and were scattered throughout space when the stars went supernova.

To simulate the effects of a supernova, the chemists held a lump of graphite under a flow of helium gas and blasted it with a laser. They expected the laser to vaporize a broad range of variously sized carbon molecules off the graphite. Instead, they found an abundance of carbon molecules with just sixty atoms. They quickly deduced that a sixty-atom carbon molecule was the most stable type of carbon molecule.

Kroto immediately imagined that the carbon atoms had formed a polyhedron (the shape of a soccer ball) with an atom at each of the sixty corners of the molecule. He named the molecule *buckminsterfullerene* in honor of Buckminster Fuller, the architect who had designed the lightweight geodesic dome supported by hexagonal lattice frameworks. Five years later, scientists synthesized buckminsterfullerene (nicknamed Buckyballs) in large enough quantities to prove that the structure of the sixty-atom carbon molecule is indeed a polyhedron, precisely as Kroto had envisioned.

SAN FRANCISCO BAY

On July 14, 1769, Spanish explorer Captain Juan Gaspar de Portolá, military governor of the Californias, headed north from San Diego with a party of sixty men on horseback to find Monterey Bay, which had been described only from ships at sea. On September 30, when de Portolá's expedition arrived at Monterey Bay and stood on its sands, they failed to recognize it. Instead de Portolá continued northward on a long, treacherous mission to search for a bay he had already bypassed.

The exhausted team got lost, climbed over San Pedro Mountain, and made camp in Pedro Valley, just fifteen miles south of modern-day

San Francisco. On November 1, 1769, one of de Portolá's men, José Francisco Ortega, led a squad of scouts on a three-day reconnaissance of the surrounding forest. Ortega sighted San Francisco Bay on his first day of scouting but assumed the inlet was the mouth of a large river. When Ortega returned to camp, de Portolá ordered further exploration of the purported estuary, and on November 4, 1769, he and his men climbed to the top of Sweeny Ridge hoping for a better view. From the ridge, de Portolá and his men realized that the extensive body of water was actually a massive bay sheltered by two peninsulas—a discovery that numerous Spanish naval expeditions of the region had failed to make.

Realizing that he had mistakenly overshot Monterey Bay by more than one hundred miles and unaware that they were the first Europeans to sight the bay, de Portolá ordered his expedition to return homeward. De Portolá ultimately located Monterey Bay and established the presidio there in 1770. Six years later, the Spanish, having finally recognized the strategic value of the huge, sheltered harbor, established the Presidio of San Francisco under the leadership of Captain Juan Bautista de Anza.

CYCLAMATES

n 1937, Michael Sveda, a 24-year-old University of Illinois chemistry graduate student performing lab work at the DuPont Company, smoked a cigarette after preparing a series of sulfamates to develop a fever-reducing drug. Sveda brushed some loose tobacco off his lips and noticed that his fingers tasted remarkably sweet.

Realizing that his fingers had been tainted by one of the sulfamates, Sveda tasted from each beaker until he located the source of the sweet-tasting chemical on his hands. That chemical was sodium cyclohexylsulfamate. Sveda also discovered that the corresponding calcium salt was equally sweet.

DuPont patented both the sodium and calcium salts of cyclohexylsulfamic acid—more commonly known as cyclamates—and later sold the patent to Abbott Laboratories, which in 1951 obtained government approval to sell the sugar-free substance as a food additive. The food industry used cyclamates as sugar substitutes in diet drinks and low-calorie desserts until 1970, when the U.S. Food and Drug Administration banned their use.

TOLLUND MAN

On May 6, 1950, brothers Viggo and Emil Højgaard, and Viggo's wife, Grethe Højgaard, were digging for peat in Tollund swamp near Bjaeldskovdal, Denmark, and found the body of a dead man lying cuddled up as if he were sleeping—with a braided leather rope tightened around his neck as a noose.

The corpse wore a serene expression on his face, a sheepskin cap, and a leather belt. The body looked so fresh that the Højgaards, convinced they had found the victim of a recent murder, contacted the police. Upon learning that the body had been found eight feet underground with no signs of recent digging, the police called in experts from the nearby Silkeborg Museum. Together, the Højgaard brothers, museum officials, and local police officers excavated the body and shipped it by horse-drawn carriage and train to the National Museum of Denmark in Copenhagen.

Archaeologists, a forensic examiner, and carbon-14 dating determined that the Tollund man had been hanged between 300 to 400 B.C.E. as part of a Semnonan religious sacrifice when he was somewhere between the ages of thirty and forty years old. The peat moss in the bog had enveloped the body, preventing oxygen from causing the corpse to deteriorate, and the tannic acid in the bog had preserved the body so well that the stubble of a beard and the hair on his head still remained. The Tollund man is considered the most well-preserved body from prehistoric times in the world.

The preserved head of the Tollund man and a recreation of his body can be viewed at the Silkeborg Museum in Silkeborg, Denmark.

PAMELA ANDERSON

I n the summer of 1989, 21-year-old Canadian fitness instructor Pamela Anderson wore a tight-fitting Labatt's beer T-shirt to a British Columbia Lions football game in Vancouver. During the game, a roving camera scanning spectators focused in on her, putting her sexy image on the Jumbotron screen and prompting the crowd to roar

with approval. After the *Vancouver Sun* reported the story with an accompanying photo, photographer Dan Ilicic created a poster featuring Anderson as a spokesmodel for Labatt's and attempted to sell the poster to the Canadian brewery. The company declined the offer, but eventually public demand compelled the company to buy one thousand posters.

Shortly afterward, freelance photographer Ken Honey took some pictures of Anderson and submitted them to *Playboy*. Publisher Hugh Hefner liked the pictures and hired Anderson to pose for the cover of the October 1989 issue. Anderson moved to Los Angeles where she landed the part of the *Tool Time* Girl on the hit television sitcom *Home Improvement*. She later starred as lifeguard C. J. Parker on the popular television series *Baywatch*.

PACEMAKER

n 1958, while working at the Chronic Disease Research Institute at the University of Buffalo in New York, Dr. Wilson Greatbatch attempted to build a device that would record the sound of a heartbeat. He accidentally used the wrong transistor to complete the circuit. The resulting circuit started emitting alternating electrical impulses.

Greatbatch immediately noticed that the pulsating pattern mimicked the human heartbeat. Realizing that this device might work as a small, implantable pacemaker for the human heart, he began experimenting to reduce the size of the device and protect it from bodily fluids.

Working in collaboration with Dr. William Chardack and Dr. Andrew Gage at the Buffalo Veterans Administration Hospital, Greatbatch developed a working model of the modern-day pacemaker. The Chardack-Greatbatch pacemaker successfully controlled a dog's heartbeat, and, in 1960, doctors effectively implanted the apparatus into the bodies of ten ailing people. The following year, Greatbatch licensed his pacemaker to Medtronic, Inc. in Minneapolis, Minnesota, and the device has been saving lives ever since as the best-selling pacemaker in the world.

VULCHITRUN TREASURE

O n December 28, 1924, brothers Todor and Nikola Tzvetanov, digging in their vineyard near the village of Vulchitrun, Bulgaria, unearthed thirteen gold vessels of various sizes and shape. Not realizing the value of their find, they attempted to cut some of the vessels to utilize them as farm tools.

The Tzvetanov brothers, in cahoots with the mayor of the village, tried to hide the treasure. They showed one of the vessels to a goldsmith Kosta Zlatarev in the nearby city of Pleven, who immediately contacted the authorities  and the National Archaeological Museum in Sofia. Museum curator Ivan Velkov immediately traveled by train to

Vulchitrun to rescue the archaeological find. The state paid the Tzvetanov brothers a reward of 1.5 million leva (approximately $10,800), but the brothers, unable to agree how to divide the money, began suing each other in court, ultimately paying the money to lawyers.

The set of gold items—weighing more than twenty-seven pounds—includes seven disks, four one-handled cups, a large two-handled vessel, and a triple bowl. Archaeologists believe that the gold utensils—dated to roughly 1500 B.C.E. during the late Bronze Age—belonged to a Thracian king who used them in religious rituals to worship the sun.

The Vulchitrun Treasure is among the most remarkable examples of ancient goldsmith work in Europe and can be seen in the National Archaeology Museum in Sofia, Bulgaria.

CHEWING GUM

n 1869, former Mexican dictator General Antonio López de Santa Anna, the man responsible thirty-three years earlier for the massacre at the Alamo in Houston, Texas, was living in exile in a leased home on Staten Island, New York. Determined to raise enough money to build an army so he could return to his country, march on Mexico City, and seize power, the exiled general asked local inventor Thomas Adams to develop a way to blend rubber with Mexican chicle—the natural gum from the sapodilla tree that people in Mexico had been chewing for centuries.

De Santa Anna hoped to reduce the cost of rubber goods and create a fierce demand for chicle, making both him and Adams wealthy men. The deposed dictator provided

Adams with a large quantity of chicle, and for more than a year, the inventor tried to use it to make tires, toys, rubber boots, and masks—but failed miserably. Adams was about to throw the entire batch of chicle into the East River, when he remembered how de Santa Anna enjoyed chewing it.

In his kitchen one evening in 1871, Adams mixed some chicle into a gummy wad and chewed on it. The chicle gum tasted smoother, softer, and more flavorful than the paraffin gums sold in the United States at the time. He made up little balls of chicle gum, wrapped them in different colored tissue papers, and packaged them in boxes, which he marketed as "Adams New York No. 1." Chicle-based chewing gum quickly became more popular than spruce gum or paraffin gum.

De Santa Anna never received a penny for the invention of chewing gum. He did, however, receive amnesty from the Mexican government, and in 1874, he returned to his country.

RAYON

n 1878, French chemist Hilaire de Chardonnet spilled a bottle of collodion while working in his photography darkroom. He neglected to clean up the spill right away, inadvertently allowing the solvent to partially evaporate, and when he did get around to sopping up the mess, the mere act of blotting the gummy puddle produced long thin strands of fiber.

Years earlier, de Chardonnet had assisted French chemist Louis Pasteur in his successful attempt to cure a disease that had killed silkworms and devastated the French silk industry. That experience helped de Chardonnet foresee  the commercial potential of inventing a synthesized silk substitute. As he cleaned up the long strands of fiber produced by the collodion, he wondered if he had indeed stumbled upon such a thing.

In 1886, after eight years of experimentation, de Chardonnet dissolved a pulp of mashed mulberry leaves (the natural food of silkworms) in ether and alcohol to produce collodion, extruded threads of fiber from the viscous solution, and used warm air to solidify the strands of his artificial silk. De Chardonnet displayed fabric made from the cellulose nitrate silk at the Paris Exposition in 1889, attracting investors to finance further development. In 1924, he trademarked the name Rayon for the new fiber. Unfortunately, cellulose nitrate was highly flammable and explosive, and the French government banned the production of de Chardonnet's artificial silk. (Today, most rayon is made by the viscose process of converting purified cellulose to xanthate.)

PLAY-DOH

n 1933, brothers Cleo and Noah McVicker of Kutol Products, a soap company in Cincinnati, Ohio, invented a doughy wallpaper cleaner that could be rolled over the decorative paper to remove soot stains caused by coal furnaces. When the advent of oil and gas furnaces made coal furnaces obsolete, sales of the wall- paper cleaner plummeted. In 1949, Cleo's son Joseph McVicker took over the floundering company.

In 1954, McVicker's sister-in-law Kay Zufall, who ran a nursery school in New Jersey, came across an article in a teacher's magazine that suggested using Kutol wallpaper cleaner as modeling clay for kids. She let her students play with the pliable compound and invited her brother to the school to witness children playing with his product.

Realizing that his invention doubled as a soft, reusable modeling compound for children, McVicker renamed his company Rainbow Crafts and instructed his uncle Noah McVicker to mix up a nontoxic batch of cream-colored wallpaper cleaner with an almond scent. Zufall and her husband Bob suggested the name "Play-Doh," and McVicker began marketing the product as a children's toy rather than a wallpaper cleaner.

First sold and demonstrated in 1956 in the toy department of Woodward & Lothrop department store in Washington, D.C., the original cream-colored Play-Doh, packaged in a twelve-ounce cardboard can, became an immediate hit. In 1957, the Rainbow Crafts Company introduced Play-Doh in blue, red, and yellow. Three years later, the company introduced the Play-Doh Fun Factory. To this day, the formula for Play-Doh remains top secret, and white-colored Play-Doh can be used to clean wallpaper.

MAGAININS

n July 1986, Dr. Michael Zasloff, a pediatrician and biochemist at the National Institutes of Health, removed an African frog's ovaries as part of a study of lung infections in children born with cystic fibrosis. He placed the frog in a tank in his laboratory to recuperate, and several days later, he noticed that the frog's surgical

wound was healing swiftly and without infection—despite the fact that the murky aquarium water teemed with bacteria.

Zasloff had operated previously on many other African frogs whose wounds had also healed quickly, but this was the first time he questioned how the wounds could possibly heal so well in such a contaminated environment.

369

He examined another recuperating frog and found no white blood cells at the site of the wound to fight off infection. Zasloff deduced that some potent chemical in the frog's skin was defending the wound from invading germs.

Investigating this phenomenon further, he ground up frog skin and isolated two peptides in the skin that impede bacteria, fungi, and protozoa. He named the new antibiotics *magainins* (Hebrew for "shields").

TOFU

egend holds that sometime after 200 B.C.E., a Chinese cook added the seaweed *nigari* to a pot of soybean soup, causing the soybean purée to curdle. The seaweed, intended as a seasoning, worked as a solidifying agent, creating a cheese-like food. Underpaid Chinese bureaucrats of the Han dynasty ate the curd as a meat substitute and became known as "tofu officials."

Around 760 C.E., Buddhist monks and priests brought tofu to Japan under the name *okabe*. In 1489, *okabe* became known in Japan as tofu but failed to gain widespread acceptance for another two centuries.

Tofu became popular in the West during the 1960s as people began seeking healthier foods and interest

in vegetarianism grew. Research began revealing the many significant health benefits provided by this nutrient-rich, plant-based food—enhancing tofu's appeal and revealing why the people of East Asia have, since ancient times, honored tofu in poems and proverbs as "meat of the fields" and "meat without a bone."

SURGICAL GLOVES

In 1889, Caroline Hampton, an operating room nurse who worked under Dr. William Stewart Halsted at the Johns Hopkins University Hospital and Medical School in Baltimore, Maryland, developed severe dermatitis on her hands and arms from repeatedly using mercuric chloride as a sterilizing solution. One day, while visiting New York, Halsted asked the Goodyear Rubber Company to make two pairs of thin rubber gloves with gauntlets that Nurse Hampton could wear to protect her hands from the mercuric chloride. If the gloves reduced his nurse's dermatitis, Halsted promised to order more.

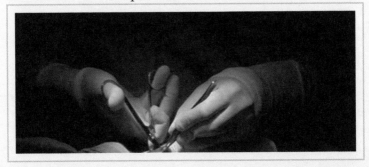

"In the autumn, on my return to town, an assistant who passed the instruments and threaded the needles was also provided with rubber gloves to wear at the operations," recalled Halsted in *Doctors: The Biography of Medicine.* "After a time, the assistants became so accustomed to working in gloves that they also wore them as operators and would remark that they seemed to be less expert with the bare hands than with the gloved hands."

Wearing the gloves cured Nurse Hampton's dermatitis, and Professor Halstead married her in 1890.

Halsted did not wear the gloves during surgery. In 1896, his protégé, Dr. Joseph Bloodgood, started using gloves himself during surgery, and soon noticed that wearing the gloves prevented infection in surgical patents, changing medical practices. Said Halsted: "Why was I so blind not to have perceived the necessity for wearing them all the time?"

ROMAN CATACOMBS

orbidden to bury their dead in burial grounds, the early Christians of Rome interred the remains in underground vaults used by the poor and built outside the city. In the fourth century, after Roman emperor Constantine embraced Christianity, Christians began burying their dead in above-ground cemeteries. In the eighth and ninth centuries, Christians moved relics of the saints from the catacombs to churches within the city walls. With the exception of a few catacombs located below martyrial churches, people generally forgot about the catacombs and ceased exploring and studying them.

On May 31, 1578, workers quarrying the volcanic stone pozzolana in the vineyard of Bartolomeo Sanchez on the Via Salaria Nuova in Rome discovered an entrance into an intact Christian catacomb containing frescoes of Bible scenes, sarcophagi, and inscriptions. Shortly after this rediscovery, the continued quarrying of the pozzolana caused a landslide, burying the catacomb.

Fifteen years later, 18-year-old Antonio Bosio, an aspiring lawyer, began investigating a number of catacombs, finding narrow passageways that linked them and discovering at least thirty entrances to other subterranean burial sites. In 1620, Bosio, having spent his life studying the catacombs scientifically and historically, finished writing a book on the catacombs entitled *Roma Sotterranea*. In the seventeenth and eighteenth centuries, fortune hunters plundered the catacombs, removing and destroying many valuable relics.

Today, the Vatican maintains the Christian catacombs in Rome.

REDDI-WIP

n 1941, Aaron "Bunny" Lapin, a 28-year-old Washington University dropout working at his father's clothing emporium in St. Louis, Missouri, went to Chicago to visit his brother-in-law, Mark Lipsky, who was in the milk business. In Lipsky's outer office sat a man trying to sell a product called Sta-Whip, a substitute whipping cream. At Lapin's suggestion, Lipsky bought the rights to Sta-Whip and gave the business to Lapin.

Lapin returned to St. Louis and made a deal with Valley Farm Dairy. The dairy would make Sta-Whip, Lapin would sell it, and they'd split the profits. Lapin convinced local bakeries to make whipped cream cakes with Sta-Whip, and within two weeks, he was

making more money with his substitute whipping cream than he was in the clothing store. To avert the slump in whipping cream sales during the summer, Lapin had a "gun" designed that drugstore soda jerks could use to squirt Sta-Whip on ice-cream sodas.

To prevent a container of Sta-Whip from spoiling before it could all be used, Lapin decided to develop a disposable aerosol can to dispense Sta-Whip. Fortunately, the process had already been developed. In 1931, Charles Goetz, a senior chemistry major at the University of Illinois, worked part-time in the Dairy Bacteriology Department, improving milk sterilization techniques. Convinced that storing milk under high gas pressure might inhibit bacterial growth, Goetz began experimenting—only to discover that milk released from a pressurized vessel foamed. Realizing that cream would become whipped cream, Goetz began seeking a gas that would not saturate the cream with its own bad flavor. At the suggestion of a local dentist, Goetz infused the cream with tasteless, odorless nitrous oxide, giving birth to aerosol whipped cream and aerosol shaving cream. In 1947, Lapin gave his aerosol whipped cream a new name—Reddi-wip.

WARFARIN

n 1933, a Wisconsin farmer dropped in on Professor Karl Paul Link at the University of Wisconsin-Madison's School of Agriculture to seek his help to figure out why local cows were bleeding to death. The farmer suspected the culprit to be the sweet clover hay he had been feeding his cattle.

Seven years later in 1940, Link and his student Harold Campbell discovered that the sweet clover had become infected with molds that metabolized the coumarin

(the organic compound that gives sweet clover its sweet vanilla-like odor) into the anticoagulant dicoumarol. In 1948, Link marketed a stronger synthesized version of dicoumarol as a rodenticide called *warfarin* (named in honor of WARF—the Wisconsin Alumni Research Foundation—and the suffix *–arin* from coumarin). Warfarin quickly became the world's best-selling and most-effective rat poison.

In 1951, a new recruit in the U.S. Army attempted suicide by taking large amounts of warfarin on several occasions. His repeated failure proved that warfarin was safe for human consumption, prompting doctors to initiate clinical trials for warfarin in preventing clotting disorders to stave off strokes and heart attacks in people. The drug was introduced in 1959 as the blood-thinning medication Coumadin.

PYREX

n 1914, Bessie Littleton's ceramic casserole dish cracked. Her husband, physicist Jesse Littleton, worked for the Corning Glass Works in Corning, New York, evaluating the properties of the new heat-resistant borosilicate glass the company used to make battery jars and signal lanterns. Bessie wondered if the heat-resistant glass that her husband studied might work for baking. Littleton sawed the bottom off a battery jar made from heat-tempered glass, gave it to his wife, and told her to bake a chocolate cake in it.

The next morning, Littleton brought the chocolate cake to work for his colleagues to prove that he—or rather his

wife—could bake food in glass. Bessie continued baking in battery jars and made custards in lamp chimneys.

Three years later, Corning launched a line of borosilicate glass ovenware under the brand name Pyrex (named for the company's first pie plate), selling 4.5 million Pyrex products by 1919. In the meantime, Corning scientists researched ways to strengthen the glass to withstand the heat of a stove top, and in 1936, the company launched a line of flame-resistant Pyrex cookware—which led to Pyrex test tubes, laboratory flasks, and hospital glassware.

PLUTO'S MOON

I n 1978, astronomer James Christy, working at the U.S. Naval Observatory in Flagstaff, Arizona, placed a photographic plate containing a picture of Pluto on a StarScan machine in an attempt to more precisely calculate Pluto's orbit. Christy immediately noticed that the images of Pluto were elongated. He dismissed the bulges as imperfections in the plate and was about to discard the photograph when the machine suddenly malfunctioned.

Christy called in a technician to repair the machine, and the technician asked Christy to stand by while he made the repairs—in case he needed Christy's assistance. While waiting, Christy studied the trapped photographic plate and

decided to look through the archives for other photographs of Pluto for comparison. The first photograph he found was labeled: "Pluto image. Elongated. Plate no good. Reject." His curiosity piqued, Christy found six more photographs showing Pluto elongated.

Based on the photos, Christy calculated that the bulge seemed to move around Pluto over 6.39 days—Pluto's rotation period. Christy deduced that the bulge was actually a moon—nearly half the size of Pluto—orbiting Pluto at the same speed as Pluto's rotation.

Christy proposed the name Charon for the moon after the mythological ferryman who carried souls across the river Acheron, one of the five mythical rivers that surrounded Pluto's underworld. Christy also chose the name Charon because the first four letters matched the name of his wife, Charlene.

Presumably, the technician fixed the StarScan machine.

SELECTED BIBLIOGRAPHY

Books

Accidents May Happen: Fifty Inventions Discovered by Mistake by Charlotte Jones (New York: Delacorte, 1998)

American Plastic: A Cultural History by Jeffrey L. Meikle (New Brunswick, NJ: Rutgers University Press, 1995)

Anaesthesia: Who Made and Developed This Great Discovery? by Gardner Quincy Colton (New York: A. G. Sherwood, 1896)

Antimicrobial Drugs: Chronicle of a Twentieth Century Medical Triumph by David Greenwood (New York: Oxford University Press, 2008)

Archaeology, Fifth Edition by Robert L. Kelly and David Hurst Thomas (Belmont, CA: Wadsworth, 2010)

The Archaeology of Measurement: Comprehending Heaven, Earth and Time in Ancient Societies, edited by Iain Morley and Colin Renfrew (New York: Cambridge University Press, 2010)

Aspartame: Physiology and Biochemistry, edited by Filer Stegink and L. J. Filer, Jr. (New York: Marcel Dekker, 1984)

The Beatles Anthology by the Beatles (San Francisco: Chronicle, 2000)

The Beatles Diary: An Intimate Day by Day History by Barry Miles (East Bridgewater, MA: World Publications, 2007)

The Beatles: Off the Record by Keith Badman (London: Omnibus Press, 2008)

Between the Lines: The Mystery of the Giant Ground Drawings of Ancient Nazca, Peru by Anthony Aveni (Austin, TX: University of Texas Press, 2000)

The Biographical Encyclopedia of American Radio edited by Christopher H. Sterling (New York: Taylor & Francis, 2011)

The Book of Tofu: Food for Mankind, Volume 1 by William Shurtleff and Akiko Aoyagi (Brookline, MA: Autumn Press, 1975)

Boyhood and Manhood Recollections: The Story of a Busy Life by Gardner Quincy Colton (New York: A. G. Sherwood, 1897)

Bright Earth: Art and the Invention of Color by Philip Ball (Chicago: The University of Chicago Press, 2003)

Burton's Microbiology for the Health Sciences, Ninth Edition by Paul G. Engelkirk and Janet L. Duben-Engelkirk (Baltimore, MD: Lippincott, Williams & Wilkins, 2011)

The Cambridge Companion to the Beatles, edited by Kenneth Womack (Cambridge, United Kingdom: Cambridge University Press, 2009)

Celebrities' Most Wanted: The Top 10 Book of Lavish Lifestyles, Tabloid Tidbits, and Superstar Oddities by Marjorie Hallenbeck-Huber (Washington, D.C.: Potomac Books, 2010)

Chicago's Sweet Candy History by Leslie Goddard (Charleston, SC: Arcadia, 2012)

Chicle: The Chewing Gum of the Americas, From the Ancient Maya to William Wrigley by Jennifer P. Mathews (Tucson, AZ: University of Arizona Press, 2009)

Cigars and Other Passions: The Biography of Edgar M. Cullman by Peter Hochstein (Victoria, Canada: Trafford Publishing, 2010)

Commemorating the Dead: Texts and Artifacts in Context, edited by Laurie Brink and Deborah Green (Berlin, Germany: de Gruyter, 2008)

A Complete Course of Lithography by Alois Senefelder (Munich, Germany: Thieneman and Gerold, 1818)

Corporate Creativity: How Innovation and Improvement Actually Happen by Alan G. Robinson and Sam Stern (San Francisco: Berret-Koehler, 1997)

Cro-Magnon: How the Ice Age Gave Birth to the First Modern Humans by Brian Fagan (New York: Bloomsbury Press, 2010)

The Dead Sea Scrolls: A Biography by John Joseph Collins (Princeton, NJ: Princeton University Press, 2013)

Discover Coloma: A Teacher's Guide by Alan Beilharz (Coloma, CA: Gold Discovery Park Association)

The Discoverers by Daniel J. Borstin (New York: Random House, 1983)

Discovery of the Elements by Mary Elvira Weeks (Easton, PA: Journal of Chemical Education, 1933)

Doctors: The Biography of Medicine by Sherwin Nuland (New York: Vintage, 1995)

The Double Helix by James Watson (New York: Touchstone Books, 2001)

Electric Welding and Welding Appliances by Herbert Carpmael (New York: D. Van Nostrand, 1920)

Emperor Qin's Terra Cotta Army: Unearthing Ancient Worlds by Michael Capek (Minneapolis: Twenty-First Century Books, 2008)

Encyclopedia of Kitchen History by Mary Ellen Snodgrass (New York: Routledge, 2004)

English Mechanic and World of Science, March 3, 1882 (Volume 34, Number 884), page 615

The Enigmas of History: Myths, Mysteries and Madness from Around the World by Alan Baker (Edinburgh, Scotland: Mainstream Publishing, 2008)

The Eureka! Moment: 100 Key Scientific Discoveries of the 20th Century by Rupert Lee (New York: Routledge, 2002)

Europe Before Rome: A Site-by-Site Tour of the Stone, Bronze, and Iron Ages by T. Douglas Price (London: Oxford University Press, 2013)

Everybody's Business: A Field Guide to the 400 Leading Companies in America by Milton Moskowitz, Robert Levering, and Michael Katz (New York: Doubleday, 1990)

Experiments and Observations on Different Kinds of Air by Joseph Priestley (London: Printed for J. Johnson, No. 72, in St. Paul's Church-Yard, 1775)

Fifteen Treasures from Bulgarian Lands by Dimiter Ovcharov, translated by Maya Pencheva (Sofia, Bulgaria: National Museum of Bulgarian Books and Polygraphy, 2003)

The First Miracle Drugs: How the Sulfa Drugs Transformed Medicine by John E. Lesch (New York: Oxford University Press, 2007)

From Gunpowder to Laser Chemistry: Discovering Chemical Reactions by Andrew Solway (Chicago: Heinemann Library, 2007)

The Gnostic Gospels by Elaine Pagels (New York: Vintage, 1979)

The Gnostic Gospels of Jesus by Marvin W. Meyer (San Francisco: HarperCollins, 2005)

Happy Accidents: Serendipity in Modern Medical Breakthroughs by Morton Meyers (New York: Arcade, 2007)

Historic London Walks by Leo Hollis (London: Cadogan Guides, 2005)

A History of Brazil, Third Edition by E. Bradford Burns (New York: Columbia University Press, 1993)

A History of the World in 100 Objects, BBC, Episode 33—"Rosetta Stone"

How the Cadillac Got Its Fins by Jack Mingo (New York: HarperCollins, 1994)

How the Hot Dog Found Its Bun: Accidental Discoveries and Unexpected Inspirations That Shape What We Eat and Drink by Josh Chetwynd (Guilford, CT: Globe Pequot Press, 2012)

"I Sweat the Flavor of Tin": Labor Activism in Early Twentieth-Century Bolivia by Robert L. Smale (Pittsburgh, PA: University of Pittsburgh Press, 2010)

In Search of Caesar, The Ultimate Caesar Salad Book by Terry D. Greenfield (Alexander Books, 1996)

Introduction to Polymer Chemistry, Third Edition by Charles E. Carraher, Jr. (Boca Raton, FL: CRC Press, 2013)

Inventing Wine: A New History of One of the World's Most Ancient Pleasures by Paul Lukacs (New York: W. W. Norton, 2012)

Laughing Gas, Viagra, and Lipitor: The Human Stories Behind the Drugs We Use by Jie Jack Li (New York: Oxford University Press, 2006)

Lee and Gaensslen's Advances in Fingerprint Technology, Third Edition, edited by Robert Ramotowski (Boca Raton, FL: CRC Press, 2013)

Lost City of the Incas: The Story of Machu Picchu and its Builders by Hiram Bingham (Lima, Peru: Librerías ABC, 1975)

The Lost World Of Pompeii by Colin Amery and Brian Curran, Jr. (London: Frances Lincoln Ltd, 2002)

Lucy: The Beginnings of Humankind by Donald Johanson and Maitland Edey (New York: Simon & Schuster, 1981)

Mammoth: The Resurrection of an Ice Age Giant by Richard Stone (Cambridge, MA: Basic Books, 2001)

Marilyn: Her Life in Her Own Words: Marilyn Monroe's Revealing Last Words and Photographs by George Barris (New York: Citadel, 1995)

Medieval Science, Technology And Medicine: An Encyclopedia, edited by Thomas F. Glick, Steven John Livesey, Faith Wallis (New York: Routledge, 2005)

The Miraculous Fever-Tree: The Cure that Changed the World by Fiammetta Rocco (London: HarperCollins, 2003)

Mistakes That Worked: 40 Familiar Inventions and How They Came to Be by Charlotte Jones (New York: Delacourte, 1994)

Mood Genes: Hunting for Origins of Mania and Depression by Samuel H. Barondes (New York: Oxford University Press, 1999)

Mysteries In History: From Prehistory to the Present by Paul Aron (Santa Barbara, CA: ABC-CLIO, 2006)

Nylon: The Story of a Fashion Revolution by Susannah Handley (Baltimore, MD: The Johns Hopkins University Press, 1999)

Of Sugar and Snow: A History of the Ice Cream Making by Jeri Quinzio (University of California Press, 2009)

Office Management: Developing Skills for Smooth Functioning by N. B. Dubey (New Delhi, India: Global India Publications, 2009)

The Origins of Everyday Things by the editors of Reader's Digest (London: Reader's Digest, 1999)

Our Story So Far (St. Paul, MN: 3M, 1977)

The 100 Most Important Chemical Compounds by Richard L. Myers (Westport, CT: Greenwood, 2007)

Panati's Extraordinary Origins of Everyday Things by Charles Panati (New York: Perennial, 1989)

Penicillin, Its Practical Application by Alexander Fleming (London: Butterworth, 1946)

Phosphorus Chemistry in Everyday Living, 2nd Edition, by A. D. F. Toy and E. N. Walsh (Washington, D.C.: American Chemical Society, 1987)

Pills, Potions and Poisons: How Drugs Work by Trevor Stone and L. Gail Darlington (New York: Oxford University Press, 2000)

Pluto Confidential: An Insider Account of the Ongoing Battles Over the Status of Pluto by Laurence A. Marschall and Stephen P. Maran (Dallas: BenBella Books, 2009)

Polythene: The Technology and Uses of Ethylene Polymers by Archibald Renfrew and Phillip Morgan (London: Iliffe & Sons, 1960)

Preventive Strikes: Women, Precancer, and Prophylactic Surgery by Ilana Löwy (Baltimore, MD: The Johns Hopkins University Press, 2010)

Psychology: Concepts and Applications by Jeffrey S. Nevid (Boston: Houghton Mifflin, 2009)

Rediscovering Antiquity: Karl Weber And The Excavation Of Herculaneum, Pompeii, And Stabiae by Christopher C. Parslow (Cambridge, United Kingdom: Cambridge University Press, 1998)

The Same Ax, Twice: Restoration and Renewal in a Throwaway Age by Howard Mansfield (Hanover, NH: University Press of New England, 2000)

Scientific American Inventions and Discoveries: All the Milestones in Ingenuity—from the Discovery of Fire to the Invention of the Microwave Oven by Rodney Carlisle (Hoboken, NJ: John Wiley & Sons, 2004)

Serendipity: Accidental Discoveries in Science by Royston M. Roberts (New York: Wiley, 1989)

Seymour/Carraher's Polymer Chemistry: Sixth Edition by Charles E. Carraher Jr. (CRC Press, 2000)

Small Things Considered: Why There Is No Perfect Design by Henry Petroski (New York: Vintage, 2003)

So Who the Heck Was Oscar Meyer? by Doug Gelbert (New York: Barricade Books, 1996)

Sundae Best: A History of Soda Fountains by Anne C. Funderburg (Bowling Green, OH: Bowling Green State University Popular Press, 2002)

Teddy Bears Past and Present: A Collector's Identification Guide by Linda Mullins (Cumberland, MD: Hobby House Press, 1986)

Transforming the Twentieth Century: Technical Innovations and Their Consequences by Vaclav Smil (New York: Oxford University Press, 2006)

Uncovering the Past: A History of Archaeology by William H. Stiebing, Jr. (Oxford, England: Oxford University Press, 1993)

Unearthing The Past: The Great Archaeological Discoveries That Have Changed History by Douglas Palmer with Paul G. Bahn and Joyce Tyldesley (London: First Lyons Press, 2005)

Why? Because We Still Like You: An Oral History of the Mickey Mouse Club by Jennifer Armstrong (New York: Grand Central Publishing, 2010)

Why Did They Name It . . . ? by Hannah Campbell (New York: Fleet, 1964)

Wiley-Blackwell Encyclopedia of Human Evolution edited by Bernard Wood (Chechester, England: Wiley-Blackwell, 2011)

Women Invent!: Two Centuries of Discoveries That Have Shaped Our World by Susan Casey (Chicago: Chicago Review Press, 1997)

The World Book Encyclopedia (Chicago: World Book, 1985)

NEWSPAPERS AND MAGAZINES

"André Cassagnes, Etch A Sketch Inventor, Is Dead at 86" by Margalit Fox, *New York Times*, February 3, 2013

"Annette Funicello Dies at 70" by Duane Byrge, *The Hollywood Reporter*, April 8, 2013

"Annette Funicello, Mouseketeer and Beach Movie Actress, Dies at 70" by Douglas Martin, *New York Times*, April 8, 2013

"August Kekulé and the Birth of the Structural Theory of Organic Chemistry in 1858," by O. T. Benfrey, *Journal of Chemical Education*, January 1958 (Volume 35), pages 21-23

"Bag Balm: Problem-Salving for All" by John Curran, Associated Press, *USA Today*, January 31, 2001

"Biblical Pool Uncovered in Jerusalem" by Thomas H. Maugh III, *Los Angeles Times*, August 9, 2005

"A Big Squirt: This Summer's Coolest Toy Can Make You Hot Just Trying to Find It" by Mike Capuzzo, *Philadelphia Inquirer*, July 1, 1991

"Botox Founder Cannot Use It On Himself" by Kounteya Sinha, *The Times of India*, February 13, 2012

"Cabral Discovers Brazil" by Richard Cavendish, *History Today* (Volume 50, Number 4), April 2000

"The Chimes of Ancient China" by Sheila Melvin, *New York Times*, April 1, 2000

"Classic Cookie Creators: The Good Old Days at Whitman's Toll House" by John Galluzzo, *South Shore Living*, November 2011

"Column One: From the Ice Comes a Mystery " by William D. Montalbano, *Los Angeles Times*, October 21, 1991

"Construction Workers Dig Up Prehistoric Bones" by Ruth Rendon, The Associated Press, January 8, 1985

"Crime Busters" by Timothy O. Bakke, *Popular Science*, February 1985, pages 82-84, 120

"The Crosbys: Literature's Most Scandalous Couple" by Peter Lyle, *The Telegraph*, June 19, 2009

"The Day DNA Met Its Match" by Rosie Mestel, *Los Angeles Times*, February 28, 2003

"Dean Martin" by Pete Martin, *Saturday Evening Post*, April 29, 1961

"Declaration of Independence Sells for $2.4 Million" by Eleanor Blau, *New York Times*, June 14, 1991

"The Development of Polymer Chemistry in America" by Dr. Carl S. Marvel, *Journal of Chemical Education*, July 1981 (Volume 58), pages 535-539

"The Discovery of Gold in California" by James W. Marshall, *Hutchings' California Magazine*, November 1857 (Volume 2, Number 5), pages 194-202

"Dippin' Dots Inventor's Aha Moment" by Laura Petrecca, *Chicago Sun-Times*, October 30, 2010

"Edison's Greatest Invention Half Century Old," *Popular Mechanics*, August 1927, pages 203-207

"Edison's Invention of the Phonograph," *The Pittsburgh Press*, April 16, 1916

"Egg McMuffin Inventor Herb Peterson Dies" by The Associated Press, March 27, 2008

"Engineer at Play: Lonnie Johnson; Rocket Science, Served Up Soggy" by William J. Broad, *New York Times*, July 31, 2001

"Eureka—South Africa Has Diamonds!" by Jade Davenport, *Creamer Media's Mining Weekly*, April 9, 2010

"The Flaky Cereal Rush" by Maggie Overfelt, *Fortune Small Business*, April 1, 2003

"Former Toledo Scientist's Sweet Discovery Ended Bitterly" by J. C. Reindl, *Toledo Blade*, February 14, 2011

"A Fortune—Frozen? Botox Inventor Dr. Jean Carruthers Never Got Patent" by Rosemary Black, *New York Daily News*, July 26, 2010

"French electrician invented Etch A Sketch" by Valerie J. Nelson, *Los Angeles Times*, February 3, 2013, A32

"The Frito" by Nicholas Lemann, *Texas Monthly*, May 1982, page 136

"From Weapon to Wonder Drug" by Johnathan Frunzi, *The Hospitalist*, February 2007

"Gardner Quincy Colton: Pioneer of Nitrous Oxide Anesthesia" by Gary B. Smith and Nicholas P. Hirsch, *Anesthesia & Analgesia*, March 1991 (Volume 72, Number 3), pages 382-391

"Goods, Graves, and Scholars: 18th-Century Archaeologists in Britain and Italy" by Nancy H. Ramage, *American Journal of Archaeology*, October 1992 (Volume 96, Number 4), pages 653-661

"Goodyear and the Strange Story of Rubber" by Richard Match, *Reader's Digest*, January 1958 (Pleasantville, New York: Reader's Digest Association, 1958)

"Hamwi Had a Cool Idea," *Lakeland Ledger*, June 4, 1975

"Harry Coover, Super Glue's Inventor, Dies at 94" by Elizabeth A. Harris, *New York*

Times, March 27, 2011

"How Did We Ever Live Without . . . " by Todd Savage, *The Chicago Tribune*, October 5, 2003

"The Ice Cream Cone," *The Newburgh Evening News*, August 28, 1968

"Ice Cream Cone-Making Is a Dayton Tradition," Associated Press, *The Portsmith Daily Times*, October 27, 1984

"In Celebration of Caesar!" by Nikki Sandelin, *Orange Coast*, July 1994, page 14

"The Invention of Saccharine," *Scientific American*, July 17, 1886, page 36

"Inventors by Accident" by Robert Cutler, *Mechanix Illustrated*, February 1950, pages 78-82

"John A. Spencer Dies; Thermostat Inventor," *New York Post*, April 2, 1937, page 11

"Julian W. Hill, Nylon's Discoverer, Dies at 91" by David Stout, *New York Times*, February 1, 1996

"Kellogg: Champion of Breakfast" by Paul Lukas, *Fortune Small Business*, March 19, 2003

"Linoleum—Another Industrial 'Accident'," *Modern Mechanix*, May 1936, pages 82-84

"Linoleum: A Chiswick Invention" by Ralph Parsons, *Brentford & Chiswick Local History Journal*, Number 5, 1996

"Lithography," *Supplement to the Fourth, Fifth, and Sixth Editions of the Encyclopaedia Britannica* (Edinburgh, Scotland: Archibald Constable and Company, 1824)

"Magainin, Shield Against Disease," *New York Times*, August 9, 1987

"Make the Most of Machu Picchu" by George Bauer, CNN, July 21, 2011

"Making Money Making Toys" by Caryne Brown, *Black Enterprise*, November 1993, pages 68-77

"Michael Sveda, the Inventor Of Cyclamates, Dies at 87" by Leslie Kaufman, *New York Times*, August 21, 1999

"Minoxidil Tests: Putting Hair Back Where It Belongs" by Robert Steinbrook, *Los Angeles Times*, September 21, 1986

"The Missing Link: The Story of Karl Paul Link" by Jerold A. Last, *Toxicological Sciences*, March 2002 (Volume 66, Issue 1), pages 4-6

"A Modern Chemist's Magic" by Boyden Sparkes, *Popular Science*, January 1923, pages 31-32

"A New Kind of Ray, a Preliminary Communication" by Wilhelm Konrad Röntgen, *Proceedings of the Würzburg Physical-Medical Society*, December 28, 1895

"'Old Salt' Doughnut Hole Inventor Tells Just How Discovery Was Made and Stomach of Earths Saved," *The Washington Post*, March 26, 1916, page ES9

"Pasadena Claims Its Slice of Burger History" by Joe Piasecki, *Los Angeles Times*, January 16, 2012

"Patents; A Chemist Who Languished in a Prefeminist-Era DuPont Lab Looks Back on Her Invention of Kevlar" by Teresa Riordan, *New York Times*, May 24, 1999

"Patents; The Man Who Gave the World Vinyl Wins a Place in the Inventors Hall of Fame" by Teresa Riordan, *New York Times*, July 24, 1995

"Phototherapy" by R. H. Dobbs and R. J. Cremer, *Archives of Disease in Childhood*, November 1975 (Volume 50, Number 11), pages 833-836

"Pompeii" by Neil Faulkner, *World Archaeology*, July 3, 1010, Issue 42

"Prehistoric Times, as illustrated by Ancient Remains and Manners and Customs of Modern Savages" by Sir John Lubbock, *The Edinburgh Review Or Critical Journal*, 1870 (Volume 132, Number 270), pages 460-461

"The Pursuit of Sweet: A History of Saccharin" by Jesse Hicks, *Chemical Heritage Magazine*, Spring 2010 (Volume 28, Number 1), pages 26-31

"Reminiscing: Who Invented Hamburger Sandwich? And What About the Cheeseburger?" by Roger M. Grace, *Metropolitan News-Enterprise*, January 8, 2004

"Reversal of Baldness in Patient Receiving Minoxidil for Hypertension" by A. R. Zappacosta, *New England Journal of Medicine*, December 18, 1980 (Volume 303, Number 25), pages 1480-1481

"Rocket Scientist Blasts Off Into Toyland" by Patricia J. Mays, Associated Press, *The Los Angeles Times*, February 7, 1999

"The Secrets of Herculaneum to be Yielded at Last," *New York Times*, November 18, 1906

"Skin Deep" by Katherine Ashenburg, *Vancouver Magazine*, June 1, 2009

"Smart Dust" by Jessica Ramirez, *The Daily Beast*, August 31, 2010

"So Botox Isn't Just Skin Deep" by Natasha Singer, *New York Times*, April 12, 2009

"Spirit of '76: $4 Purchase His Declaration of Financial Independence," Press News Services, *The Pittsburgh Press*, April 3, 1991

"Talk of the Town," *The New Yorker*, December 19, 1942

"Temple of Mithras Comes Home" by Maev Kennedy, *The Guardian*, January 19, 2012

"Thai Antiquities, Resting Uneasily" by Jori Finkel, *New York Times*, February 17, 2008

"They Built This City: Mill City Museum Celebrates Minneapolis' Riverfront, Industry, People" by Peg Meier, *Minneapolis Star Tribune*, September 6, 2003

"This Month in Physics History: February 1968: The Discovery of Pulsars Announced," *APS News*, February 2006 (Volume 15, Number 2)

"True Size of Pool of Siloam Discovered Due to Sewer Blockage" by Nadav Shragai and Haaretz Correspondent, *Haartez*, December 23, 2005

"Unknown Van Gogh Pops Up In Wisconsin" by Frank James and Alan Artner, *Chicago Tribune*, January 9, 1991

"Van Gogh Still Life Draws Lively $1.43 Million" by George Papajohn, *Chicago Tribune*, March 11, 1991

"The Venus of Milo," *The Open Court*, September 1913 (Volume 27, Number 9), pages 513-544

"Was He the Eggman?" by Gregory Beyer, *New York Times*, April 8, 2007

"Windover's Ancient 'Bog People' Made History" by Robert Hughes, *Space Coast Daily*, January 13, 2013

INDEX

Anderson, Pamela, 357

Archimedes' Principle, 41

Aspartame, 53

Aurignac Cave, 271

Austin Mastodons, 59

Avon, 235

Bag Balm, 43

Bakelite, 75

Ban Chiang Artifacts, 311

Batteries, 317

Beatles, 161

Big Bang, 327

Birth Control Pill, 255

Biskupin Village, 263

Black Hills Mammoths, 201

Blue Jeans, 119

Botox, 13

Bra, 241

Brandy, 333

Brazil, 167

Bubble Gum, 9

Bubble Wrap, 313

Buckyballs, 349

Caesar Salad, 147

Calendar, 117

California Gold Rush, 287

Cartesian Plane, 153

Cellophane, 19

Celluloid, 183

Ceres, 213

Champagne, 217

Cheeseburger, 345

Chemotherapy, 285

Chewing Gum, 363

Chicken Cholera Vaccine, 17

Chocolate Chip Cookies, 193

Classical Conditioning, 175

Cobb Salad, 257

Coca-Cola, 11

Cro-Magnon Man, 337

Cyclamates, 353

Daguerreotype, 133

Dead Sea Scrolls, 95

Declaration of Independence, 129

Dippin' Dots, 319

Dixie Cups, 91

DNA Structure, 293

Doughnuts, 101

Dry Cleaning, 281

Eggs Benedict, 67

Electric Welding, 243

Etch A Sketch, 105

Eureka Diamond, 209

Ex-Lax, 269

Fingerprinting, 261

Folsom Site, 299

Frisbee, 39

Fritos Corn Chips, 159

Funicello, Annette, 221

Gnostic Gospels, 27

Granola and Corn Flakes, 179

Gravity, 77

Green Giant, 87

Gunpowder and Fireworks, 81

Hall and Oates, 291

Herculaneum, 107

Ice-Cream Cone, 239

Ice-Cream Soda, 307

Infant Jaundice Cure, 141

Inkjet Printer, 169

Insulin, 237

Iodine, 185

Ivory Soap, 57

Johnston Atoll, 321

Kevlar, 289

Kleenex, 207

Kool-Aid, 275

Kotex, 115

Lascaux Cave Paintings, 55

Lea & Perrins Worcestershire Sauce, 79

Lindow Man, 143

Linoleum, 121

Liquid Paper, 347

Liquorice Allsorts, 301

Lithium for Bipolar Disorder, 309

Lithography, 315

Lucy, 187

Machu Picchu, 71

Magainins, 369

Martin and Lewis, 45

Matches, 219

Mauve, 297

Microwave Oven, 229

Milk Duds, 251

Milk-Bone Dog Biscuits, 227

Molecular Structure, 225

Monroe, Marilyn, 97

Mr. Coffee Machine, 61

Nazca Lines, 177

Neanderthal Man, 277

Nitrous Oxide as an Anesthetic, 123

Noxzema, 35

Nuclear Fission, 259

Nylon, 329

Ötzi the Iceman, 85

Oxygen, 89

Pacemaker, 359

Penicillin, 231

Petri Dish, 31

Phonograph, 189

Phosphorus, 111

Piggy Banks, 325

Play-Doh, 367

Pluto's Moon, 383

Polyethylene, 253

Pompeii, 109

Pool of Siloam, 37

Pop-Up Toaster, 163

Popcorn, 83

Popsicle, 199

Post-it Notes, 171

Potato Chips, 21

Potosí, 127

Prussian Blue, 343

Pulsars, 305

Pyrex, 381

Q-tips, 195

Quinine, 197

Radioactivity, 181

"Rain", 265

Rayon, 365

Reddi-wip, 377

Regenerative Circuit, 149

Rogaine, 335

Roman Catacombs, 375

Rosetta Stone, 157

Ruby Falls, 245

S.O.S Steel Wool Pads, 73

Saccharine, 131

Safety Glass, 151

San Francisco Bay, 351

Scotch Tape, 23

Scotchgard, 295

Silly Putty, 69

Slinky, 145

Sloan's Liniment, 139

Smallpox Vaccine, 165

Smart Dust, 99

Stainless Steel, 65

"Still Life With Flowers", 331

Sulfa Drugs, 49

Super Glue, 203

Super Soaker, 173

Surgical Gloves, 373

Tabasco Pepper Sauce, 25

Taung Child, 233

Tea, 33

Tea Bags, 279

Teddy Bears, 247

Teflon, 211

Telephone, 47

Temple of Mithras, 137

Templo Mayor, 223

Terracotta Warriors, 15

Thermostatic Switch, 267

Tinker Toys, 283

Tofu, 371

Tollund Man, 355

Tomb of Marquis Yi of Zeng, 191

Turtle Wax, 155

Uranus, 103

Vacuum Cleaner, 273

Vaseline, 135

Velcro, 323

Venus de Milo, 303

Vinyl, 51

Vulcanized Rubber, 29

Vulchitrun Treasure, 361

Warfarin, 379

Watermark, 215

Western Hemisphere, 215

Wheaties, 93

Whistling Tea Kettle, 341

Windover Archaeological Site, 113

Wish-Bone Salad Dressing, 249

Wooly Willy, 205

World Wide Web, 339

X-Rays, 63

ACKNOWLEDGEMENTS

At Hallmark Gift Books, I am grateful to my editor, Kimberly Schworm Acosta, for her keen editorial eye and her unbridled enthusiasm for this book. I am also deeply thankful to editor Megan Langford; ace copyeditors Amber Stenger, Amy McCuen, and Jennifer Clark; designer and illustrator Brian Pilachowski; editorial strategist Delia Berrigan Fakis; awesome art director Chris Opheim; my agent Laurie Abkemeier; researcher Debbie Green; research assistant Howard Gershen; and my manager Barb North.

Thanks to Howard Chrisman, Amy St. Eve, Lauren Chrisman, Emily Chrisman, Brett Chrisman, Curt Jones, Andy and Desiree Steinberg, and Bob Epstein. Above all, all my love to Debbie, Ashley, and Julia.

Grateful thanks to the artists, photographers, picture collectors, and private collectors who have contributed to this book:

Page 9 (Bubble gum): Photograph by Joey Green. "Dubble Bubble" is a registered trademark of Concord Confections Inc. Used with permission.

Page 11 (Coca-Cola): Photograph by Joey Green. "Coca-Cola" is a registered trademark of the Coca-Cola Company.

Page 15 (Terracotta Warriors): Photograph Copyright © 1989 by Deborah Green. Used with permission.

Page 17 (Chicken Cholera Vaccine): Photograph of Louis Pasteur, Courtesy of the Library of Congress, Prints and Photographs Division, Reproduction number LC-DIG-ggbain-14544.

Page 19 (Cellophane): Photograph Copyright © 1923 DuPont. Used with permission.

Page 25 (Tabasco Pepper Sauce): Photograph courtesy of McIlhenny Company. The TABASCO® marks, bottle and label designs are registered trademarks and servicemarks exclusively of McIlhenny Company, Avery Island, Louisiana 70513. Used with permission. Visit www.tabasco.com.

Page 27 (Gnostic Gospels): Photograph by Wolfgang Rieger. Public Domain.

Page 35 (Noxzema): Photograph by Joey Green. "Noxzema" is a registered trademark of Unilever. Used with permission.

Page 37 (Pool of Siloam): Photography Copyright © 2009 by Michael Schroeder. Used with permission. Visit www.michaelschroeder.com.

Page 41 (Archimedes' Principle): "Archimedes Thoughtful" (1620) by Domenico Feti, Gemäldegaleria Alte Meister, Dresden, Germany.

Page 43 (Bag Balm): Photograph by Joey Green. "Bag Balm" is a registered trademark of the Dairy

Association Co, Inc. Used with permission.

Page 45 (Martin and Lewis): Courtesy of Robert Barnes Archives.

Page 55 (Lascaux Cave Paintings): Photograph by Norbert Aujoulet; Image courtesy of Ministry of Culture and Communications/National Center of Prehistory, France.

Page 57 (Ivory): Photograph by Joey Green. "Ivory" is registered trademark of Procter & Gamble. Used with permission.

Page 59 (Austin Mastadons): Courtesy of the Smithsonian Institution.

Page 61 (Mr. Coffee Machine): Photograph by Joey Green. "Mr. Coffee" is a registered trademark of Sunbeam Products. Used with permission.

Page 127 (Potosí): Engraving of Potosí by Bernard Lens, printed as inset on Map of South America by Herman Moll, London, circa 1709-1720. Courtesy of the John Carter Brown Library at Brown University.

Page 129 (Declaration of Independence): Broadside printed by John Dunlap, Philadelphia. Courtesy of the Library of Congress Rare Books and Special Collections Division.

Page 131 (Saccharine): Photograph by Joey Green. "Sweet 'N Low" is a registered trademark of Cumberland Packing Corp. Used with permission.

Page 133 (Daguerreotype): Daguerreotype of Louis Daguerre, photographed by Jean-Baptiste Sabatier-Blot (1844). Collection of George Eastman House, International Museum of Photography and Film.

Page 135 (Vaseline): Photograph by Joey Green. "Vaseline" is a registered trademark of Unilever. Used with permission.

Page 139 (Sloan's Liniment): Photograph by Joey Green. "Sloan's" is a registered trademark of Lee Pharmaceuticals, Inc. Used with permission.

Page 145 (Slinky): Photograph by Joey Green. "Slinky" is a registered trademark of Poof-Slinky, Inc. Used with permission.

Page 155 (Turtle Wax): Photograph by Joey Green. "Turtle Wax" and "Hard Shell Finish" are registered trademarks of Turtle Wax, Inc. Used with permission.

Page 159 (Fritos): Photograph by Joey Green. "Fritos" is a registered trademark of Frito-Lay North America, Inc. Used with permission.

Page 165 (Smallpox Vaccine): WHO/Novosti, Courtesy of National Library of Medicine.

Page 167 (Brazil): Map from The Voyage of Pedro Álvares Cabral, Hakluyt Society, England, 1937.

Page 175 (Classical Conditioning): Photograph of Ivan Pavlov. Courtesy of the National Library of Medicine.

Page 177 (Nazca Lines): Photograph Copyright © 1987 by Deborah Green. Used with permission.

Page 179 (Granola and Corn Flakes): Photograph by Joey Green. "Kellogg" is a registered trademark of Kellogg Co. Used with permission.

Page 181 (Radioactivity): Art Explosion.

Page 187 (Lucy): Courtesy of the Houston Museum of Natural Science.

Page 191 (Tomb of Marquis Yi of Zeng): Photograph Copyright © 2010 by Gary Todd. Used with permission. Visit www.GaryLeeTodd.com (Chinese and World History).

Page 195 (Q-tips): Art Explosion.

Page 197 (Quinine): Illustration by Franz Eugen *Köhler, Köhler's Medizinal-Pflanzen,* 1897, courtesy of the United States Forest Service.

Page 199 (Popsicle): Photograph by Joey Green. "Popsicle" is a registered trademark of Unilever. Used with permission.

Page 201 (Black Hills Mammoths): Courtesy of the Smithsonian Institution.

Page 205 (Wooly Willy): Photograph Copyright © Patch Products. "Wooly Willy" is a registered trademark of Patch Products. Used with permission.

Page 207 (Kleenex): "Kleenex" is a registered trademark of Kimberly-Clark Worldwide, Inc. © KCWW. Used with permission.

Page 209 (Eureka Diamond): Photograph by Carina Steyn, Copyright © 2013 De Beers Consolidated Mines Ltd. Used with permission.

Page 213 (Ceres): NASA.

Page 215 (Watermarks): Art Explosion.

Page 227 (Milk-Bone): Photograph by Joey Green. "Milk-Bone" is a registered trademark of Del-Monte Corporation. Used with permission.

Page 231 (Penicillin): Photograph of Sir Alexander Fleming. Cover of Bulletin of Lederie Laboratories, Volume 12, Number 1, Spring 1944. Courtesy of the National Library of Medicine.

Page 233 (Taung Child): Photograph by Chip Clark, courtesy of the Smithsonian Institution.

Page 237 (Insulin): "Drs. Banting and Best in the Laboratory," April 21, 1921, Public Domain, Courtesy of the National Library of Medicine.

Page 243 (Electric Welding): Thomson Electric Welding Company Catalog, circa 1890.

Page 245 (Ruby Falls): Photograph Copyright © 2013 Ruby Falls. Used with permission.

Page 251 (Milk Duds): Photograph by Joey Green. "Milk Duds" are a registered trademark of The Hershey Company. Used with permission.

Page 259 (Nuclear Fission): Mushroom cloud during Operation Crossroads, July 1946. Courtesy of the Library of Congress, Prints and Photographs Division, Reproduction number LC-DIG-ds-02948.

Page 263 (Biskupin Village): Copyright © 2012 by Aleksandra Wolska. Public Domain.

Page 271 (Aurignac Cave): Photograph by Totor-22. Public Domain.

Page 275 (Kool-Aid): Photograph by Joey Green. "Kool-Aid" and the Kool-Aid Man Design are registered trademarks of Kraft Foods and are used with permission.

Page 277 (Neanderthal Man): Photograph by Chip Clark, Smithsonian Institution.

Page 285 (Chemotherapy): Art Explosion.

Page 287 (California Gold Rush): Daguerreotype by R. H. Vance (1850) of Sutter's Mill with James W. Marshall in the foreground. Courtesy of the Library of Congress, Prints and Photographs Division, Reproduction number LC-USZ62-137164.

Page 291 (Hall and Oates): Courtesy of Robert Barnes Archive.

Page 299 (Folsom Site): U.S. Department of the Interior, Bureau of Land Management.

Page 305 (Pulsars): NASA.

Page 307 (Ice-Cream Soda): Photograph by Alan Fisher (1936). Courtesy of the Library of Congress, Prints and Photographs Division, Reproduction number LC-USZ62-113825.

Page 311 (Ban Chiang Artifacts): Photograph Copyright © 2011 by Corrado Prever. Used with permission. Visit www.artphotoasia.net

Page 319 (Dippin' Dots): Photograph Copyright © 2012 by Dippin' Dots LLC. "Dippin' Dots" is a

registered trademark of Dippin' Dots LLC. Used with permission.

Page 321 (Johnston Atoll): Photograph by D. Lindsay Hayes, Courtesy of U.S. Fish and Wildlife Services.

Page 327 (Big Bang): NASA.

Page 329 (Nylon): Photograph of Julian Hill by DuPont. Used with permission.

Page 331 ("Still Life With Flowers"): "Self-Portrait" by Vincent van Gogh (1889), Collection of Mr. and Mrs. John Hay Whitney, courtesy of the National Gallery of Art.

Page 337 (Cro-Magnon Man): Photograph courtesy of the Smithsonian Institution,

Human Origins Program.

Page 341 (Wheaties): Photograph by General Mills. "Wheaties" is a registered trademark of General Mills. Used with permission.

Page 347 (Liquid Paper): Photograph by Joey Green. "Liquid Paper" is a registered trademark of Berol Corporation. Used with permission. Visit www.liquidpaper.com

Page 351 (San Francisco Bay): Art Explosion.

Page 355 (Tollund Man): Photograph by Sven Rosborn. Public Domain.

Page 357 (Pamela Anderson): Photograph Copyright © 1989 by Dann Ilicic. Used with permission. Visit www.wowbranding.com

Page 361 (Vulchitrun Treasure): Courtesy of National Institute of Archaeology with Museum, Sofia, Bulgaria. Used with permission.

Page 363 (Chewing Gum): Photograph by Joey Green. "Chiclets" is a registered trademark used with permission.

Page 369 (Magainins): Art Explosion.

Page 373 (Surgical Gloves): Art Explosion.

Page 375 (Roman Catacombs): Illustration by Adolphe Rouargue, 1861.

Page 377 (Reddi-wip): Photograph by Joey Green. "Reddi-wip" is a registered trademark of ConAgra Foods, Omaha, Nebraska. Used with permission.

Page 383 (Pluto's Moon): Artist's Conception of Pluto and Charon by NASA, ESA, and G. Bacon (StScl).

Page 409 (Author): Photograph Copyright © 2012 by Debbie Green. Used with permission.

All other photographs by Joey Green.

Illustrations on pages 13, 21, 29, 31, 33, 39, 47, 51, 65, 67, 77, 93, 101, 111, 113, 117, 149, 163, 171, 189, 193, 225, 229, 239, 241, 247, 265, 273, 279, 307, 317, 323, 325, 343, 349, and 379 by Brian Pilachowski.

ABOUT THE AUTHOR

Joey Green, a former contributing editor to *National Lampoon* and a former advertising copywriter at J. Walter Thompson, is the author of more than fifty (yes, fifty) books, including *Contrary to Popular Belief*, *Clean It! Fix It! Eat It!*, the best-selling *Joey Green's Magic Brands* series, *The Mad Scientist Handbook* series, and *You Know You've Reached Middle Age If . . .* —to name just a few.

Joey has appeared on dozens of national television shows, including *The Tonight Show with Jay Leno*, *Good Morning America*, and *The View*. He has been profiled in the *New York Times*, *People magazine*, the *Los Angeles Times*, the *Washington Post*, and *USA Today*, and he has been interviewed on hundreds of radio shows.

A native of Miami, Florida, and a graduate of Cornell University (where he was the political cartoonist on the *Cornell Daily Sun* and founded the campus humor magazine, the *Cornell Lunatic*, still published to this very day), Joey lives in Los Angeles.

Visit Joey Green at www.joeygreen.com.

If you have enjoyed this book
or it has touched your life in some way,
we would love to hear from you.

Please send your comments to:
Hallmark Book Feedback
P.O. Box 419034
Mail Drop 100
Kansas City, MO 64141

Or e-mail us at:
booknotes@hallmark.com